DESIGN THEN QUILT

A DYNAMIC GUIDE TO CREATING STUNNING MODERN QUILTS

DESIGN THEN QUILT

A DYNAMIC GUIDE TO CREATING STUNNING MODERN QUILTS

SCHIFFER CRAFT

4880 Lower Valley Road • Atglen, PA 19310

IRENE RODERICK

Other Schiffer Craft Books on Related Subjects:

The Quilting Power Grid: A Design Skillbook for Beginning Modern Quilters, with 50 Example Projects, Sandra Sider, ISBN 978-0-7643-6550-8

Unconventional & Unexpected, 2nd Edition: American Quilts Below the Radar, 1950–2000, Roderick Kiracofe, ISBN 978-0-7643-6302-3

Art Quilts Unfolding: 50 Years of Innovation, Sandra Sider, ed.; Nancy Bavor, Lisa Ellis, Martha Sielman, SAQA (Studio Art Quilt Associates, Inc.), ISBN 978-0-7643-5626-1

Packaged by BlueRed Press Ltd. 2022
Designed by Insight Design Concepts Ltd.
All photography by the author except:
Amanda Ruden, p. 96 (BR); Donna Blalock, p. 96 (TL); Marilyn Knepp, p. 96 (BL); Mary Hogan, p. 95 (BR); Petra Reeves, cover, pp. 4, 18 (BL), 101, 105, 111, 113, 115, 117, 121, 134, 135 TL, 136, 137, 138, 139, 140, 141 (BOTH), 143 (BOTH), 144, 147, 150, 151, 152, 154, 156, 157, 158, 159, 160, 162, 163, 164, 165, 166, 167, 168, 169, 170, 171, 172, 173, 174, 175, 176.
Type set in Montserrat and Bebas

Library of Congress Control Number: 2024941450

ISBN: 978-0-7643-6877-6

Printed by 1010 Printing International Ltd (China):

Published by Schiffer Craft
An imprint of Schiffer Publishing, Ltd.
4880 Lower Valley Road
Atglen, PA 19310
Phone: (610) 593-1777; Fax: (610) 593-2002
Email: Info@schifferbooks.com
Web: www.schifferbooks.com

For our complete selection of fine books on this and related subjects, please visit our website at www.schifferbooks.com. You may also write for a free catalog.

Schiffer Publishing's titles are available at special discounts for bulk purchases for sales promotions or premiums. Special editions, including personalized covers, corporate imprints, and excerpts, can be created in large quantities for special needs. For more information, contact the publisher.

We are always looking for people to write books on new and related subjects. If you have an idea for a book, please contact us at proposals@schifferbooks.com.

I dedicate this book to my four sons, Marshall, Travis, Taylor, and Max, for their lifelong patience and support.

Measurements

I dance in imperial measurements, not metric!

Some of the metric equivalents need rounding up or down.

If you cannot work in imperial, use this chart to see the exact equivalents, and round to a figure you can sensibly measure.

METRIC CONVERSION CHART

inch	mm
1/8	3.175
1/4	6.35
3/8	9.525
1/2	12.7
5/8	15.875
3/4	19.05
7/8	22.225
1	25.4
2	50.8
3	76.2
4	101.6
5	127

Contents

Irene and her tiny house

Waiting In Line at SXSW

INTRODUCTION

When I teach improvisational quilting workshops, many students tell me they are hungry for a serious discussion of design. They are interested in learning what constitutes good design and how to use it in their art practices. Because of this interest, I decided to offer a workshop for quilters that teaches design as used by visual artists and graphic designers but focuses on quilting. Most books about quilt design talk about how to design a specific quilt or a particular pattern and do not address in an educational way how design elements and principles work to create visual impact in a work of art.

This text defines design and how to use it, or not, when creating a quilt. In the first sections of the book, I introduce the elements of design such as line, shape, form, and color. Then I talk about the principles of design such as balance, variety, movement, and harmony. As I define each of the different subjects, I use my own quilts and those of my workshop students as illustrations and examples.

In the next section, I focus on putting the elements into practice. A quilt is constructed of three layers, and each can be an opportunity for creativity. I discuss techniques and how each uses different design elements in distinct ways. I delve into quilt construction, quilting techniques, and the importance of consciously using good design in every step of the quilting process to make the best art we can!

I have been an artist for most of my life. I have painted and crafted for over 50 years, mostly in my home while raising four sons and working in retail and administrative positions. I returned to school at the age of 46, earning a bachelor's of

fine arts degree from the University of Texas at Austin, then a master's of fine arts degree from the California Institute of the Arts. Currently I split my time between working in my studio and teaching workshops. I work in my studio eight hours a day, six days a week when possible, and I teach workshops on improvisational quilting techniques, creativity, and design both in person and online. I even wrote a book on my signature style of improvisational quilting, a technique called "Dancing with the Wall."

Danielle Acorta working on her "Dancing with the Wall" quilt

DESIGN PRINCIPLES GIVE US A WAY TO TALK ABOUT ART

DESIGN PRINCIPLES GIVE US A WAY TO ASSESS ART

DESIGN PRINCIPLES GIVE US A WAY TO ACCESS ART

WHAT IS DESIGN?

The dictionary definition of DESIGN is "an arrangement of lines or shapes created to form a pattern or decoration." THAT is "pattern" design. There's also GRAPHIC DESIGN, which is about designing for commercial endeavors. What I want to discuss is VISUAL DESIGN or the arrangement and manipulation of elements across the surface of a visual composition. We are making textile arts in the forms of quilts, weavings, felting, embroideries, and soft sculptures. In order to make our art shine, it is important to use every method at our fingertips to create our most aesthetically pleasing and strongly spirited work possible.

We know that the concepts of design have been around since ancient Greeks based the proportions of architecture on the golden ratio (more on this later). There is disagreement, though, about the actual origins of humans using "rules" for surface decoration. Cave paintings tell stories based on arrangement of figures and animals. The Egyptians used hieroglyphics arranged in particular patterns to convey meaning and record their culture. It isn't until the rise of graphic design in the 1930s that the elements and principles of design became part of the discussion about how visual elements are arranged on a surface.

Metholithic cave painting, Spain, circa 32,000 BCE

The elements we use today to analyze our designs are recently developed, and we need to remember that for centuries, artists made works of great art without knowing or discussing these particular rules. I bring this up because I hear students talk about the "rules" of design they have been taught. We need to remember that the design principles are tools for us to use when we want, not rules we must follow.

Many of us were taught the "rule of thirds." We also learned that it is more pleasing to use an odd number of objects in a composition. A large item placed smack dab in the center of a quilt is WRONG! We were told to never place an object close to the edge because it leads our eyes off the page. I have read in many instructional books on design that there are "good" and "bad" arrangements of elements. That there are "pleasing" and "unfortunate" compositions. I want to discuss the conventions that we have been using in art classes for the past 90 years in order to determine this goodness or badness. I also want to discuss the possibility that we can break these "rules" and still make dynamic, meaningful, aesthetically beautiful works of art. But first, we need to know the rules so that we can break them with knowledge and purpose to convey our own unique messages through our creative endeavors.

Derse Verse, 2024

RULE OF THIRDS: A design technique in which the composition is divided into thirds, both horizontally and vertically. This creates four intersections and nine rectangles. The main element of the design is positioned on an intersection of the grid. A counterpoint is then placed on the opposing intersection for balance. Aesthetically pleasing and easy to do.

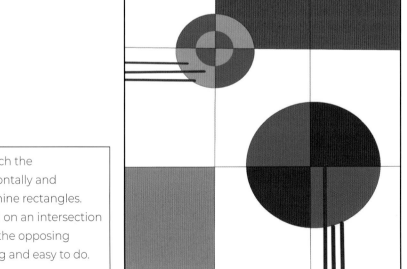

WHAT ARE THESE RULES?

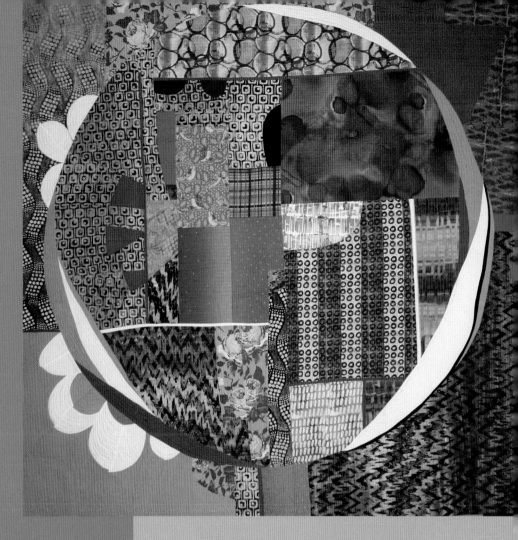

WHAT ARE THE ELEMENTS AND PRINCIPLES OF DESIGN AND WHAT'S THE DIFFERENCE?

THE
ELEMENTS
OF DESIGN

LINE
SHAPE
FORM
TEXTURE
COLOR
VALUE
SIZE
PATTERN

The **Elements** of **Design** are the **PARTS** that define the visual; that is, the tools and components used to create a composition. They are the building blocks.

CONTRAST
BALANCE
EMPHASIS
PROPORTION
MOVEMENT
UNITY/
HARMONY
REPETITION
RHYTHM
VARIETY

The **Principles** of **Design** are about **HOW** these elements are used to create a visual expression and convey a message.

THE ELEMENTS OF DESIGN vs. THE PRINCIPLES OF DESIGN

The **Elements** of design are the **PARTS** that make up an image. There are disputes over how many design elements there are and what they are, but I learned that there are eight, and that's what I will introduce to you. These are the building blocks for visual art. They combine together to create a picture or sculpture or, really, everything we see.

Sometimes it's easier to grasp a concept when it's attributed to a familiar object in the world.

LET'S LOOK AT A LEAF:

The outline of a leaf is an implied **line**.

The outline forms a **shape** that is filled in and defines the body of the leaf.

The shape then has depth (albeit mostly thin) and becomes a **form**.

The surface has **texture** that gives us a clue to what kind of leaf it may be.

The shape has **color** particular to that leaf at any given time.

The shape has a color **value** that can single it out among all the other leaves.

The leaf shape has **patterning**.

The leaf shape is a size by itself and has **scale** when thrown in with other leaves or flowers or tree limbs.

Image page 12: *Spring Storm*

LINE

SHAPE
AND
COLOR

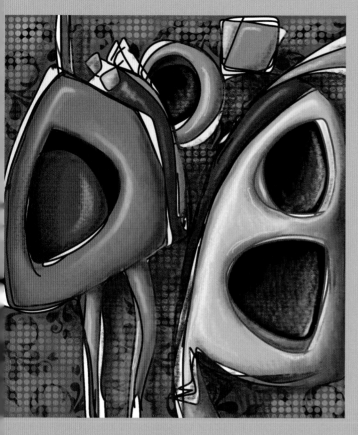

FORM

TEXTURE

LINE

Lines are the most basic design element. Every composition is created of lines in various forms. The definition of a line is a straight or curved continuous extent of length without breadth. In visual designs we know that most lines need some breadth to be seen. Lines are basic but they do a lot of work!

WHAT LINES CAN DO

Lines create contour and forms: a line can meander around and find its way back to connect to its beginning and voilà! creates a shape.

Lines are directional: follow a line and it will take you somewhere.

Lines create movement: we just followed a line to go somewhere.

Lines can create depth: Thoughtful use of lines in different widths, lengths, colors, and values creates the illusion of depth. Think how a bolder, darker, warmer line will come forward in a composition and a thinner, lighter, cooler-colored line will appear to recede.

KINDS OF LINES

Outlines: Lines identify the edges of shapes or forms. When a line connects back to its other end, it creates a shape.

Contour: Lines can be used to define contours within shapes.

Gesture: Lines naturally depict movement. They lead the eyes at all times.

Sketch: A line jotted down quickly creates a sketch and depicts impressions.

Calligraphic: Most written languages use lines.

Implied: A line that doesn't link up visually can still create eye movement. Our eyes will follow a directional line across the points of triangles, or behind other objects or across a compositional surface, to link up with another line.

Notice the lines pictured here.

Which ones are calming?
Do any feel more stable than others?
Are there some that are more fun?
Which ones are full of energy?
Do any remind you of calligraphy?
Do any look like the lines you draw when you are sketching?

LINES HAVE MEANING

Vertical: An upright line depicts stability and strength. Think about pillars in front of a building. The vertical line is also associated with how we stand with our feet planted on the ground, which takes strength and energy.

Horizontal: A horizontal line is calming. The horizon line at the beach is just as relaxing as we are when we are lying down.

Curves: A curved line creates movement in a design. Our eyes love to follow a meandering curve to a new destination more slowly than a straight line.

Diagonal: The most energetic form of a straight line is the diagonal! This direction is exciting and active.

Radiating: Another curved line that depicts action and excitement is the line that begins in the center and radiates out, like a whirlpool or pinwheel or lollipop!

Wiggly: A wiggly line is just fun. Almost always. Except when it is a snake, maybe. Then it can be a little scary.

Lines I use as "components" in my quilts. Each has a personality and stands alone also as a shape.

Spring Storm (detail)

Notice the lines in these quilts. Below, the lines fill space. In the quilt on the right, the lines are used both as outlines and to create movement. In the quilt above, the "lightning" line creates energy. The name of the quilt is *Spring Storm*. That line is definitely lightning!

Conversation (detail)

Line Drawing Landscape (detail)

Snoopy

I love the personalities of lines. When you are creating a composition, think about the overall emotion you are creating and find the lines you need. Are they rigid and straight? Are they curved and sensuous? Are they wiggly and fun? Or are they pointy and scary?

Spotlight

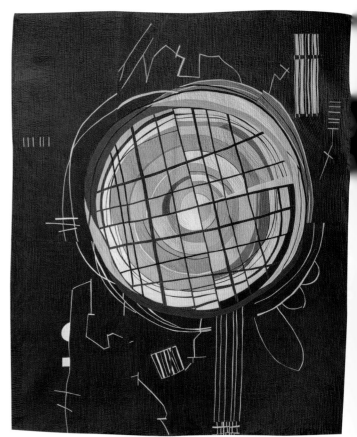

In these two quilts, it is apparent how the lines are the main elements in each design. In S*noopy* (above), the lines twirl and interact to create movement and, unfortunately, the nose of Snoopy. To the right is *Spotlight*. Whimsical and dynamic lines create an energy field surrounding the "light." Lines that cross the spotlight create the illusion of physicality. It's fun to see how these lines each perform in the quilts—and all in very spare, mostly neutral palettes.

SHAPE

Shapes are defined by lines. Lines whose ends meet up actually make all shapes. Shapes don't have any depth and therefore are two-dimensional, but they can contain color, value, and texture. They can create movement just like lines do. Shapes have personalities too, just like lines. A tall, thin shape can be elegant. A short, wide shape may depict stability. Triangles create movement and can depict many familiar objects. Circles are good at implying movement because we all know they can roll!

Those are simple shapes! Shapes are also silhouettes or maps or expressions! Shapes are areas of color.

When shapes are spaced across a composition, the space between the shapes also becomes a shape. The between shape is normally the background for the shapes, but sometimes the between shapes become a figure as well. When the amount of space filled by the background becomes almost equal to the space filled by the figures, a 50/50 figure-ground relationship is created. The fun thing about 50/50 relationships is that you can change what is the figure and what is the ground when you look at it (sometimes you need to squint!) The figure-ground relationship is merely that—the relationship between a figure and its background. Usually a figure has a definite shape, whereas the background does not but looks as if it is behind the figure. The figure normally appears in front of the ground and closer to the viewer. When a shape is clearly a figure and the background clearly a background, the composition is more stable and less confusing (unlike this explanation). In the case of a two-color quilt (*facing page*), the shapes made by the two colors create an overall pattern that feels stable because it is simple to visualize and does not try to be a figure on a ground.

In the quilt on the bottom right, the shapes of fabric offcuts from garment making create wonderful shapes to play with. In choosing to use different colors behind them, shapes are created in the background as well. The background shapes are as interesting as the figure shapes but are differentiated by the patterning of the fabrics versus the solid fabrics. This quilt is all about shapes and the play between them.

Woodcut

Australian Shapes

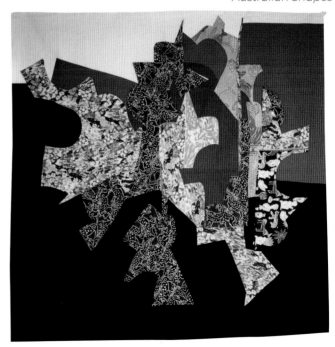

FORM

Forms are shapes with dimension! They have tops and bottoms and sides and are capable of casting a shadow. Think cubes, pyramids, spheres and cones . . . and just about everything you see in any direction you look. The world is made up of forms. But most quilts are not. This is not to say that quilted fabrics cannot be made into three-dimensional objects. I love making and receiving pincushions, which I consider small fabric sculptures. Some 3-D elements are used on quilt tops such as yo-yos and prairie points. Adventurous quilters are turning their quilts into dimensional sculptural pieces. Even trapunto techniques (depicted at right and bottom right) create a more dimensional look by placing extra loft behind areas of the quilt. We think of shape as being flat and form as having volume.

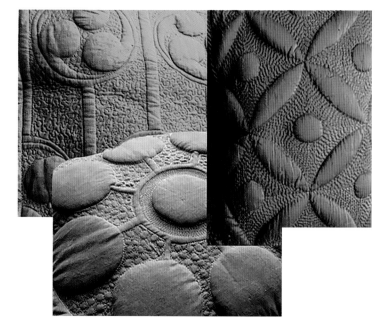

TEXTURE

Texture is the feel, the finish, the surface, the appearance of a form. It can be real and tactile. You can touch it and feel it. Or it can be implied and visual only. Think of all those fake wood grain ceramic tiles. They look like wood but are smooth, cool ceramic surfaces.

Texture provides interest and variety. In quilting, visual texture can be created by the use of printed fabrics. In the photograph below, it is evident how prints are works of art themselves and how different patterns created different types of texture. The other texture in quilting is, of course, quilting! In the images at right, the top photograph shows hand quilting and below it is machine quilting.

The other texture in quilting is, of course, quilting! A quilt needs stitching to hold together the three layers of top, filler, and backing, and each stitching type creates a different look and feel.

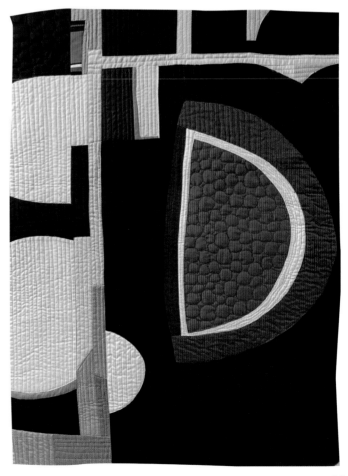

COLOR

Color is a huge subject. Systems have been created around how it works and how it's used. Many books have been written about it. I want to keep my discussion less intense. Let's start with the scientific definition. Color is the response of the eye to differing wavelengths of light. This occurs when light passes into the eye and is converted by cones and rods into signals that then go to our brains to be interpreted as color.

The objects we see possess a property of producing different colors as a result of the way they reflect light. It freaks me out to imagine every object as not really being a "real" color. Color "feels" so tangible to me that it's hard for me to know it's a trick of light.

Let's review the basic color terminology.

Hue: The name for a color in its purest form, such as red or blue or turquoise

Value: The lightness or darkness of a hue, also called saturation or brightness or intensity

Shade:	To make a shade, add black to the hue
Tone:	To make a tone, add gray to the hue
Tint:	To make a tint, add white to the hue

Primary Colors: Pure Hues. Combined, they create every other color:
Red, Yellow, Blue (analog), Magenta, Yellow, Cyan (digital)

Secondary Colors: Created by mixing two primary colors
Orange (red + yellow), Green (yellow + blue), Purple (blue + red)

Tertiary Colors: Created by mixing secondary colors
Yellow Orange, Red Orange, Red Violet, Blue Violet, Yellow Green, Blue Green

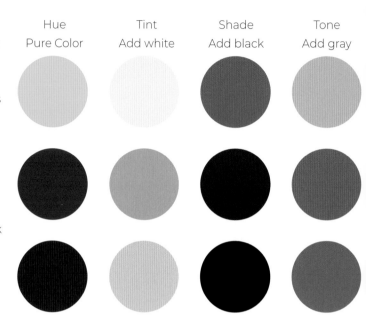

Hue — Pure Color | Tint — Add white | Shade — Add black | Tone — Add gray

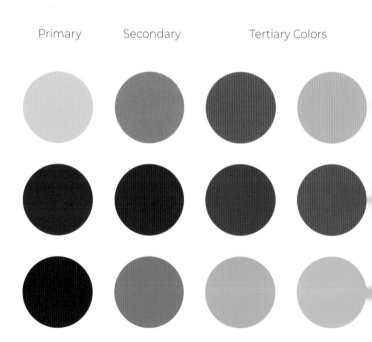

Primary | Secondary | Tertiary Colors

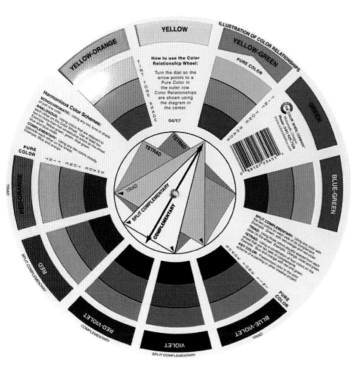

A handy color wheel showing hues, shades, tints, and tones. The center circle defines color combinations that have been identified as relevant for pleasing design.

Thoughts on Color

I am always surprised at the anxiety with which many quilters approach color. Color to me is intuitive, and I don't usually choose a palette for a new quilt design. I begin with a color that is at hand, and add others as I create, reacting to what is already in my design. I know through years of painting that a color on one side of my composition may not react the same way on the other side. It is because of this that I like to pick colors as I compose rather than try to force a prechosen palette to play nicely across the entire design. When I am ready to add a color, I will often pull out 10–50 fabrics in a hue and audition them all. I hold them up in front of my design wall one at a time until I find the perfect one. There are so many subtleties in color that each fabric will react differently with what I have already used and in that particular part of the design.

I also love to mix slightly different values and temperatures of the same hue to create interest and depth. If I run out of a particular fabric, I don't buy more but use what I have in my stash that is close in color. The light in my studio one winter was so bad that I thought I was using the same red in a quilt, only to realize when I saw it hanging at a quilt show that it contains about eight different varieties of that color. And I loved the way it made the design so much more interesting.

I encourage you to choose colors that you love and not to worry about all the rules. If a color combination looks good to you, it is.

REALLY GOOD COLOR COMBOS

Monochromatic: Single hue using tones, tints, and shades to create design.

Analogous: Neighbors on the color wheel.

Complementary: Opposites on the color wheel.

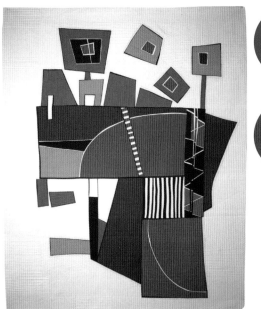

Triadic: Three colors equally spaced on the color wheel.

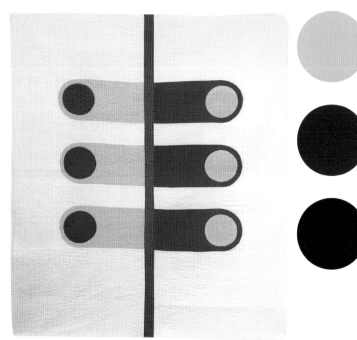

THEY ARE SHIFTY LITTLE FELLOWS

They change depending on their close friends.

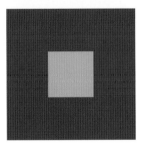

A color can change in temperature and intensity depending whom it's hanging with.

Colors change depending on the colors next to or around them and on the light in which they are viewed. This is what makes color so difficult to pin down. Colors are different in bright daylight than they are at dusk. When the light is waning, all colors gray out. Colors on your computer screen are different than colors of paint. Colors that mix nicely in paint don't play as nicely in fabric dyes. Some people are color blind and can't differentiate between greens and reds. Colors are perceived differently even if we aren't color blind. My best friend thinks her chair is green, but I know it is blue! This is also why we shouldn't take the study of color so seriously.
So, that is what color IS. Now let's look at what color can DO. The saying is that "value does all the work and color has all the fun," but I can't differentiate a "color" from its value. So let's just say a color is a color is a color. A pink may be a light red, but it's still pink to me.

So what can color do?

Color can:
- Create depth
- Create a mood
- Create an emotion
- Create a temperature
- Create a time and place
- Create dominance
- Create a memory
- Create movement

More about color . . .

Colors have temperatures that have been assigned by counterparts in the physical world. Water in nature is normally coolish. Ice is blue. Purples are the color of shadows. Therefore, also cool. Green is associated with forests. Reds and yellows and oranges are the colors of heat. Because of these inherent temperatures, colors can convey everything from emotions to spatial relationships. We talk about anger as "seeing red." Because we associate water with the beach, blues calm us. When you are looking into the distance, atmospheric conditions cause the mountains to look blue or purple or gray.

Some of our relationships with color perception come from social norms and our own experiences. Pink in recent history is associated with girly, bubble gum, Pepto Bismol? Turquoise will always remind me of the American West because that is where the stone is predominant. Blue and gray bring back memories of high school. Orange and black, red and green, pastels, red and pink—all holidays in the US. Interestingly enough, black now reminds me of Portland and Seattle because of the Goth movement. We can't escape these associations because they are deeply ingrained in our psyches. Our color choices come from all the experiences we have had. Even though Nancy Crow wants us to love brown, the house I grew up in was all browns and beiges. No color anywhere. The wood paneling was brown. The furniture was brown. The kitchen was all brown. The bathrooms were brown. I know that chocolate and coffee are also brown, but being enveloped in brown in a home that was oppressive makes it hard to love brown.

Remember also that our color preferences change over time. In today's world, I understand that the fashion and interior design industries determine what our favorite new colors will be. Remember when we all disliked orange? I cringe when I remember the era of dusty rose and Williamsburg blue.

Studies tell us which colors we prefer to live with. I recently found a study of color that assigns feelings to colors. If you study these, it's easy to see that these relationships come from social norms. Kings wore purples because the dyes were expensive and unstable. Brown is dependable and friendly because it was a dye easy to make and everyone wore it, including your friendly shopkeeper. White is purity because it denotes cleanliness—and virginity. Unsoiled. It's not complicated. You can understand why I titled these quilts *Best Friends* (*below*) and *Royalty* (*right*). The colors lead to the relationships of the figures in the quilts. Don't the two friends look friendlier and down to earth? The three kings seem majestic in their royal purple.

Red	passion, energy
Yellow	happy, upbeat
Green	stability, harmony
Blue	peace
Purple	luxury
Black	power, elegance, edgy
White	purity, simplicity
Brown	dependability

Best Friends

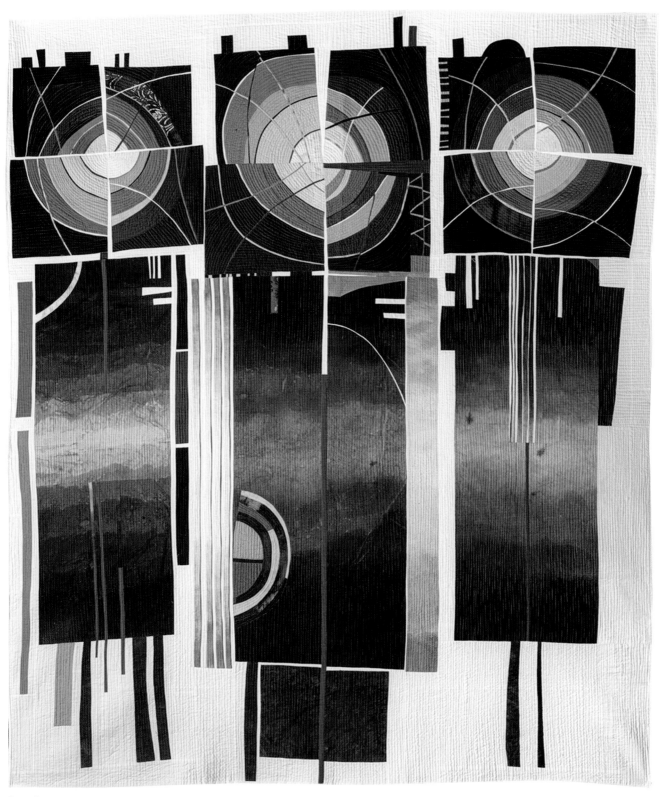

Royalty

In a composition, color can also be used to create dominance. Strong, bright colors jump out from a design if contrasted with a neutral background, either light or dark. Warm colors will visually pop against a cool-colored ground, and cool colors will recede when used with a warm ground.

In asymmetric compositions, color is a common method of obtaining balance. Because brighter colors jump forward, they also demand attention. If one side of the design is feeling heavy, adding a touch of a bright color on the other side works well.

These two quilts are balanced through the use of color. *The Kiss* uses pops of hot red orange in three places to balance. *Karaoke* uses white. We don't think of white as a color, but in this case, it works to open up a bit of light in the lower part of the design.

The Kiss

Karaoke

Don't be afraid of color. Play with it and experiment with it and enjoy it! See how it can create emotions or depth or movement. Let it be uncomfortable and see how interesting it can be. There are no rules about how to use color. You make your own rules. I think color is one area that can begin to change how we look at contemporary quilting.

Interactions of colors can be used to spectacular effect. There are some colors that seem to repel each other. There are some colors that vibrate when next to each other. Some colors seem unattractive.

Colors that seem to repel each other and create discomfort often create interest. These are my favorite combinations, and this tension can be a useful tool.

VALUE

Value is the lightness or darkness of a color in relation to other colors. We often speak of value as inherent to a hue, and yes, every hue also has an inherent value based on the light spectrum. Yellow is the lightest hue because it is closest to white, and violet is the darkest because it is closest to black.

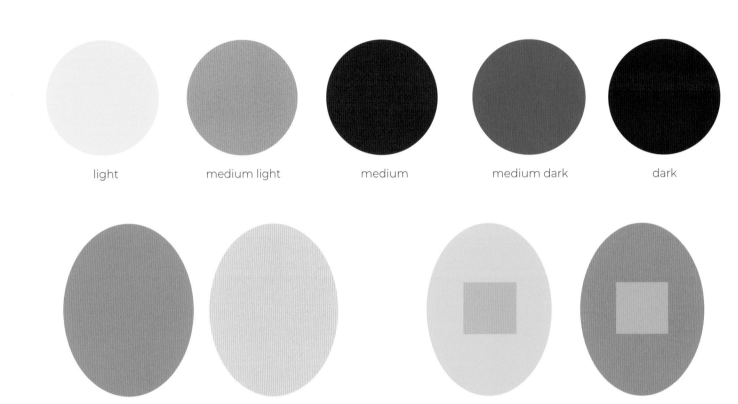

light | medium light | medium | medium dark | dark

Intensity and saturation can affect value (dark yellow is darker than light violet!).

The intensity and saturation of the same color can affect value. The green squares are the same color.

The gray scale below shows how the value of a color changes against other values. The center gray squares are all the same value. Pretty amazing!

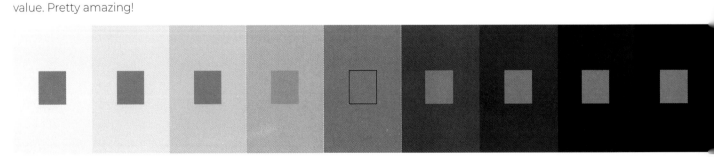

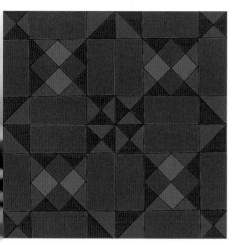  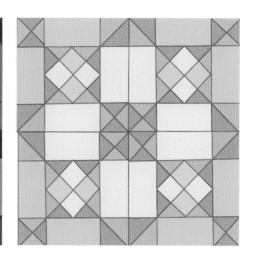

To make a design shine, use different values. If you use only dark values, the composition lacks definition. If only light values, the design looks washed out. To create depth, always use varying values, regardless of colors you choose. To determine values of your fabrics, turn your phone photo to black and white. Sometimes it's very surprising!

If you squint at this quilt, you can see how the lightest stripe and square pop out. The values create a sense of depth as the darker stripes recede.

I Vant To Be Alone

This quilt relies on value entirely for its success.

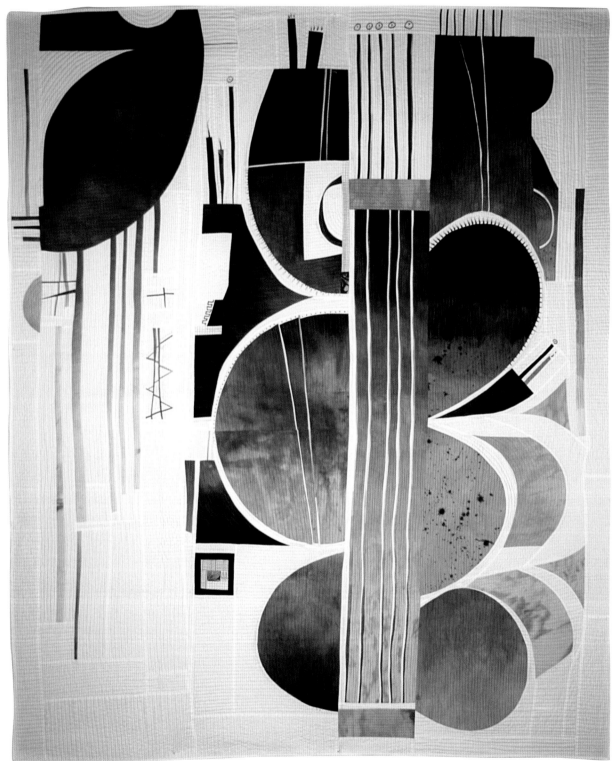

Viola da Gamba

If you doubt the power of value, just look how my "no free" disappears because I was paying more attention to color than value. In the photos below, changing the position of the values creates an entirely different effect! It's fascinating to me how

the entire structure of the quilt feels different when the dark points extend out. I can feel movement in a different way than when the light points extend out. That one feels more circular and flowerlike.

SIZE/SCALE

Size and scale are similar but not the same.

Size is the actual physical size of a shape. It may be 2" x 4" or 2' x 4'. It is descriptive and measurable.

Scale is all about comparison. Shapes are relative in size on the basis of each other and the design area. Scale is about proportion within a composition and also in the physical world.

If you look at the quilt below, it is apparent that it is quite large for a quilt (7' x 23'). We can know this because of its relative size to other items in the room.

Scale can be crucial in developing depth in a design. Larger objects look closer to us, smaller ones farther away. Color and value can also create depth, but our eyes and experience determine that larger is closer.

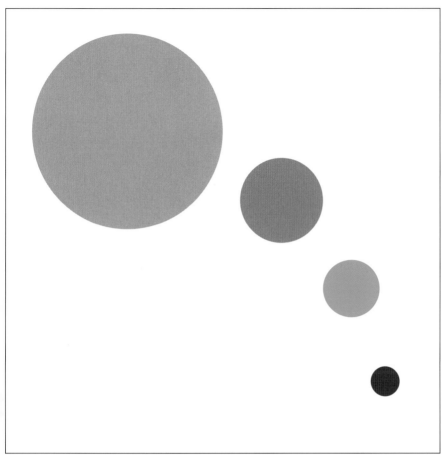

The large circle feels as if it is closer to us than the smaller circles, even if the distance between them is the same and the colors indicate otherwise.

In these three illustrations, the design is at different scales. Each creates a different effect. The larger-scale elements explode from the frame, and the smallest seems very far away.

Notice also how each scale creates differing negative space. The midscale design is not as dynamic or interesting as the other two.

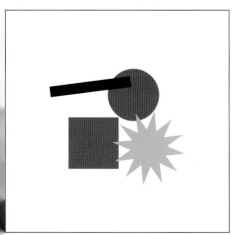

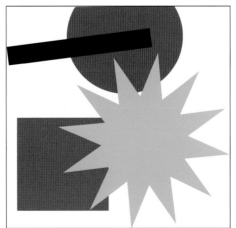

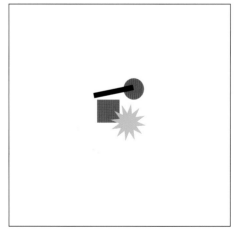

PATTERN

Pattern as an element of design can be defined in terms of repetition of shapes or lines or forms. We are talking about visual pattern, not a pattern used for making a garment or structure. Pattern can be defined as design, decoration, arrangement, or sequence, or a combination of these. Repetition creates rhythm and visual interest in a composition.

Many quilts use traditional blocks in repetition. In the quilt below, notice how the squares in the centers of the circles create a pattern. The backgrounds of color also create a pattern that our eyes follow across the surface. The circular rings, though, are the dominant element because the black-and-white repetition in a ring is a pattern easily recognized by the human eye.

Around the Block

Three quilts on this page show varying methods of using circular shapes to create pattern. In the double wedding ring quilt, they intertwine. In *Send in the Clowns*, they line up in rows, and the red "noses" reinforce the larger pattern. The third design uses circles spread out across the surface in a regular pattern supported by the contrasting ground pattern.

Double Wedding Ring

Send in the Clowns

Constructivism

Triangle Mini

The wonky elements in this mini quilt play off the traditional "nine-patch" quilt pattern and create a whimsical design.

CONTRAST

BALANCE

EMPHASIS

PROPORTION

MOVEMENT

UNITY/ HARMONY

REPETITION

RHYTHM

VARIETY

THE PRINCIPLES OF DESIGN

THE PRINCIPLES OF DESIGN ARE THE HOW OF DESIGN. IT IS THE WAY WE ARRANGE AND USE OUR ELEMENTS TO CREATE DYNAMIC VISUAL EXPERIENCES.

These PRINCIPLES are a way to give structure and meaning to art. When they work together, a design can achieve its goal and be more aesthetically pleasing. They are the fundamental ideas that serve as the foundation to all design. These principles provide guidance and give artists important points to consider. Design principles are also a way to teach us how to think about a design, because they give us a way to talk about visual compositions. They create a vocabulary for discussion and critique. One of the most important activities in an art practice is being able to step back and cast a critical eye on your work. You also need to ask others to give feedback. We often get so caught up in our work that we may not be able to "see" it clearly. When we can experience our work through someone else's eyes, it can open our eyes to problems we might not have realized are there, and also helps us see new possibilities.

Design principles help guide and steer a design throughout the design process. At each point of the process, it is possible to consider and review a design. We don't want to wait until the composition is finished to assess its quality. As we create our design, it is important to be super aware of each step of our progress. Is what we are doing working? Did that last color do what you wanted it to do? Have I unbalanced the entire composition, and if so, how can I fix it? Another crucial part of the process is sitting and just looking. Going through the design principles in your head as you study your work can help focus your thoughts and determine what is most strong and what might need some more work.

BUT . . . Rather than merely asking, "Is this a good design?," an artist needs to ask, "Is this a good design in relation to my ideas/intent?" You may have not had a clear concept when you started your composition, and overall design is therefore the most relevant assessment. When I start an improv quilt, I often have no idea what I want to make. I work intuitively and prefer to see what comes out of my hands at any given time. Later I

can look back and recognize what was on my mind and what I was experiencing when I made the quilt. But if you want to communicate a message in your art, it's important to verify that your design elements are working to communicate with your audience.

Remember that these principles are guides, not rules. Guides lead you toward something and don't demand anything. Some principles may not be relevant for your art piece. You may know that you want a symmetrical whole-cloth quilt. Color and quality of stitching might be the only relevant considerations. Because they are not RULES, you can embrace them or ignore them. Many of us want to know exactly what is right and what is wrong and would prefer some hard-core structure to follow. We find safety in rules. Educators in the 1950s–1990s presented the principles as rules, and those of us who were students during that era still have difficulty putting a focal point smack dab in the center of a composition. Or having two figures instead of the accepted odd number. Or even having a focal point. As the art world has evolved, the old rules are being tossed out the window as new, fresh ideas are needed to capture the attention of jaded customers.

So why am I writing this book on design if everything is being tossed? Because I feel it's important to know the guidelines. It's important to have the vocabulary to be able to discuss art. Design practice may have changed, but the concepts are still today's foundation of critique and aesthetic decisions. We make thousands of decisions as we make our art, and we need to learn which ones work better than others. As we create, we should be asking a lot of "What if" questions. We should be experimenting and taking risks and learning what we want our art to be. It's only through trial and error that we find out how our unique aesthetic looks. Every choice you make becomes part of your voice and separates your work from all others. Design principles give you the tools to talk about your choices, why you made them, and how these choices can make your designs more effective.

CONTRAST

Contrast is all about difference. Differences in color, in scale, in temperature, in saturation, in shapes, in styles, in values. Any kind of contrast creates interest. If all the elements in your composition are similar, there isn't anywhere for the viewer's gaze to grab ont o. Let's be frank: if there is no contrast, it's boring. Let's look at some types of contrast:

Scale: big and small

Contrasts in scale are often used to create depth and dimension. Elements that are larger in a composition come forward, and smaller ones recede.

Shape: curves, angles, squares, lines

Different shapes aren't necessary to create interest, but designs that include varying types of shapes are more interesting. Contrast might not be in types of shapes, but within types of shapes as well. Many different widths or textures of line can be just as effective.

Texture: prints, solids

The visual contrast of patterned fabrics and solid fabrics is clear and can be used to stunning effect. Even different scales used within patterned fabrics creates a spark and movement.

Color: hue, temperature, saturation

Difference in color, of course, is a common way to create an interesting composition. Complementary colors are renowned for being a most pleasing combination. These colors that reside across the color wheel from each other make each other pop! They are usually opposites in temperature as well.

Value: light and dark

Light and dark. Black and white. Bright and dull. All of these contrasting characteristics of color are one of the most effective methods to create interest in a design.

In these quilts I have used contrasts in texture, color temperature, and scale. In the top left quilt, the contrast between the patterned fabrics and the solids makes a more cohesive yet interesting design. *Spring Storm* (*top*) uses complementary colors and temperature changes as well. *Chatter* (*bottom*) is a mixture of large figures and smaller silhouettes to create interesting interactions between the elements.

Spring Storm

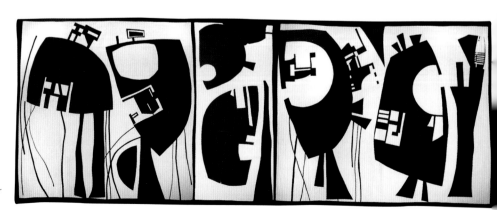

Chatter

BALANCE

Balance is one of the simpler principles to understand. We are born with an innate sense of balance, and we begin our balancing when we first learn to sit upright. Being unbalanced is uncomfortable to us. We feel we are toppling over, or, when referring to our minds, we are not in control of our sanity. If we feel unbalanced, we will automatically adjust our environment to get everything back to stable. Physical balance is related to gravity. Think about standing in front of a structure and something heavy is on top of it. We sense it can fall and injure us. Our fear of falling to the ground is the main reason we feel uncomfortable. But how does that relate to visual balance?

Balance in a composition refers to the distribution of the visual weight of the elements in a design so that it doesn't appear to topple over or tip to one side. We assign physical balance perceptions to our design balance. As human beings, we are mostly symmetrical, with a center axis and limbs extending out. It's not surprising that we are drawn to designs that are symmetrical. That is how we look at each other! Asymmetric balance might be thought of as unbalanced, but visually there are ways to make a composition appear balanced even though the main element may be off-center. The trick is to distribute the visual weight across the design so that it appears to be balanced. It can actually be demonstrated how this can happen with a physical tool. Let's look at a fulcrum and see how it works. In the physical world, we know that equal weights on each end of a fulcrum will balance nicely whether the weight is situated in one entity or more than one. We know that the density of an object determines its weight, not its size. We know that we need to move a heavier entity toward the fulcrum's balance point if we want to balance a lighter entity. It's easy to see how lighter objects will slide down toward the heavier object when the balance is off. These physical rules of physics hold true for visual weight as well. But when we are concerned only with the visual, there are more things to consider. In the physical world, a red object isn't any heavier than the exact same one that is green. Nor is a fuzzy object actually heavier than a smooth one. When referring to visual weight, determination of the impact on the eye and brain is how we differentiate the weight of elements. We "know" that a round object on a slant will roll downhill, and this implied movement spikes our interest. A bolt of lightning is definitely full of excitement! A weird, interesting shape stops

us since we want to see what it is. Colorful objects seem more fun than those that are a somber gray. Why is this? Something about the way our brains work.

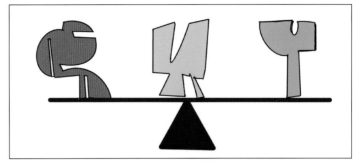

Symmetrical: equal size, evenly distributed

Balance through placement

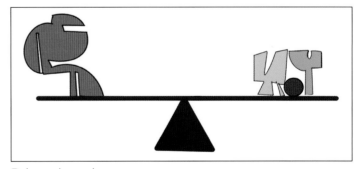

Balance by scale

Unbalanced!

THERE ARE FOUR TYPES OF VISUAL BALANCE DEFINED IN THE WORLD OF DESIGN. THEY ARE SYMMETRICAL, ASYMMETRICAL, RADIAL, AND CRYSTALLOGRAPHIC.

Symmetrical or formal balance can be on the horizontal axis or the vertical axis or both. This is also called bilateral symmetry, because one side is the mirror image of the other (top to bottom or right to left or both). Also called "formal" balance, this type is considered stable or static. It imparts power and stability and strength. Think of the US Capitol building or an altar in a cathedral. Symmetry is calming and comfortable.

Shell Game

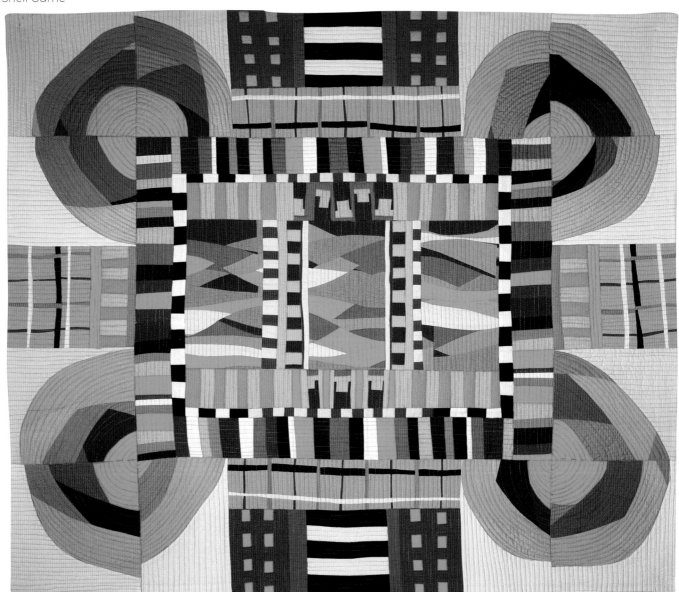

Voltron

Human beings are "asymmetrically symmetric," because our left side and right side do not perfectly mirror each other but contain slight differences. Most objects that are handmade are not perfectly symmetrical, and that makes them much more interesting. Something too perfect looks machine-made. These two quilts may appear symmetrical, but they have many differences on each side. These differences invite the viewer to stop and figure out what they are.

Informal or **asymmetric** balance is achieved by arranging design elements in ways that give us the feeling of balance. This can be done with dissimilar objects that have equal visual weight or, to put it another way, have equal attraction visually. Don't let the idea of informality make you think it is easier to achieve than symmetrical balance. It's actually more complicated and takes much planning and, sometimes, experimentation.

We create visual balance through arrangement of elements, their sizes, shapes, texture, value, and color. First, we need to realize there are elements that are intrinsically HEAVY and there are elements that are intrinsically LIGHTER.

ELEMENTS THAT ARE INTRINSICALLY HEAVY:

DARK COLORS
LARGE SHAPES
INTRICATE SHAPES
HEAVILY TEXTURED

ELEMENTS THAT ARE INTRINSICALLY LIGHT:

LIGHT COLORS
SMALL SHAPES
SIMPLE SHAPES
SMOOTH OR LIGHTLY TEXTURED

To balance a composition, you can use these simple concepts:

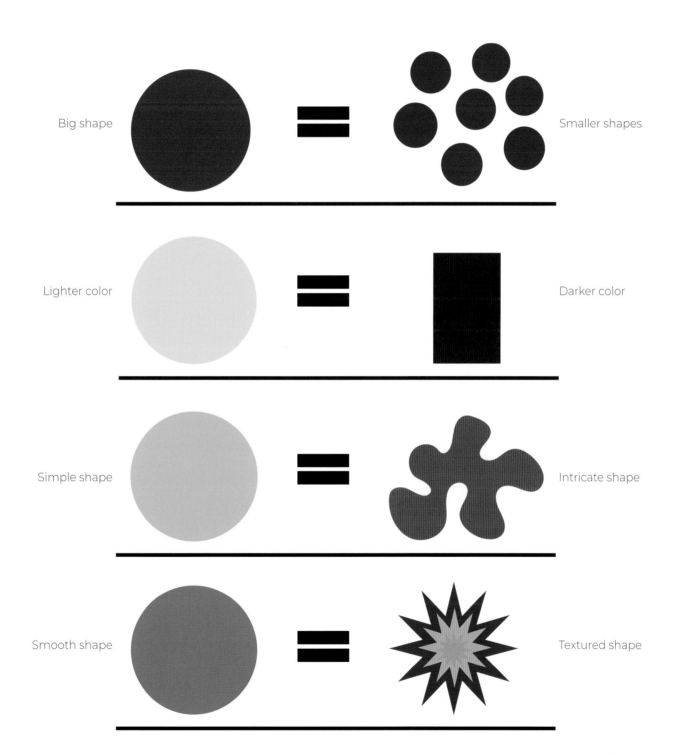

Big shape = Smaller shapes

Lighter color = Darker color

Simple shape = Intricate shape

Smooth shape = Textured shape

Movement is another aspect to consider when balancing a composition. An element that looks as if it is in motion, or is about to be, is more eye-catching than a nice, stable element.

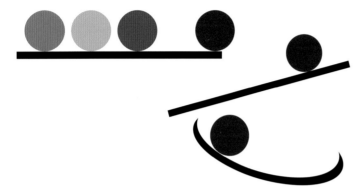

Radial balance is just what it sounds like. Elements radiate or circle out from the center of a composition or various points across the design. Think sunflowers or whirlpools. We feel comfortable with radial balance because we see it so often in nature.

These quilts have radial balance because each of them has implied direction, leading from the center of the quilt to the edges. *She's Lost Control Again* (*below*) is the strongest and most obvious, but *Limbo* (*opposite, top*) and *Venus of Willendorf* (*opposite, bottom left*) appear to swirl around a central point. This type of balance is very active and invigorating. We can almost feel the movements that each creates.

The Juggler by Lin Elmo

In Lin Elmo's quilt (*above*), she has placed the red circles very carefully and strategically so that they create an interesting tension. Some are balancing on the tip of a line, ready to fall at the slightest touch. One is seemingly rolling back and forth in a bowl shape; two are flanking and squeezing a box. The one at the bottom of the quilt is equally important to imply motion. It has actually fallen and gotten lodged next to a line.

She's Lost Control Again

Limbo

The last type of balance is **crystallographic** or "all-over" patterning. As quilters, we have long been aware of this type of balance. Quilts made from traditional quilt blocks are definitely crystallographic! There is no center of interest or one point of emphasis, but focus on the entire surface as a single pattern.

Venus of Willendorf

Fractured

53

EMPHASIS

Emphasis is special importance, value, or prominence given to something. It's associated with intensity of expression or vigor! Wow! That's a lot of emphasis to live up to and create in our compositions. We create emphasis in our art to attract attention and give meaning to what we make.

There are many ways to attract attention to our work by making one or more elements make the viewer stop and look. I hear students talk about the necessity to create a focal point that draws attention. This is definitely a grabber, but be aware that you can use more than one area or element as focal points. Or you can emphasize the whole over the parts and not use a focal point at all. This is common in block-based quilts where the all-over pattern is more important, as in the quilt to the right. The quilt below is also overall, but not traditional.

Contrast in color, value, scale, and even shape can create emphasis. It's easy to see in these quilts. In the quilt at lower right, the orange and red smaller circles (which resemble pimentos) jump out from the field of green larger circles.

Untitled by Amanda Bernay

Big Eyes

Green Magnetism

How about creating emphasis by isolation or placement? Placing an element close to the center of a composition creates immediate attention. In many designs, a centrally placed element is supported by actual or implied lines leading our eyes to it. As humans, though, in viewing anything, we first look directly in front of our eyes—where we expect another person's eyes to be. My series of *Guardian* quilts, including the quilt below, seems to depict figures that demand respect because they are placed front and center in the compositions. The "head" of each figure is where we expect to see a head, and the shapes reinforce that idea. The figures are also isolated against a neutral background. When we separate one element from the rest of the composition, we draw emphasis to that item. This also plays into emphasis by perception. We are drawn to images that mirror ourselves. Our eyes follow lines. We look first to "eyes" and "hearts." We look first to the center. All of this is based on our perception of ourselves.

Below, *Mr. Bojangles, Dance* has a front and center point of emphasis. He draws attention by placement and isolation from the ground and dark color. The surrounding linework either emanates from him or points to him.

Mr Bojangles, Dance

Empty Speech Bubbles

Above, the central panel of vertical lines in *Empty Speech Bubbles* takes center stage. The curved lines seem to swirl around it, and its density creates a powerful center form.

Celebration of Indigo

PROPORTION

Proportion is about relationships. It's about ratios. If the ratio between one element to another is what it should be, we are comfortable. The relationship is working for us.

Here we see a bird in a tree. The tree is tree size and the bird is bird size. What if we play with the proportions and make the bird tree-size? It becomes quite confusing. The ratio between the size of the bird and the tree is not what we are familiar with.

When we talked about size and scale, we mentioned that size is measurable in the physical world. Scale is about the relationship of size to other elements, including the physical world. Human scale is also called "life-size." The relationship is based on the size of a person. All scale is actually based on the same concept. Small scale is small because it is not as large as life-size. When the scale is quite small, we refer to it as miniature scale. Large scale can be slightly large, or even colossal and gigantic! Throughout the scaling up or down of a design, though, it is important to keep the proportions correct. The proportion is about the ratio of the parts to one another. In the silly drawings above, the bird's proportion did not have the correct scale.

The Greeks were obsessed with beauty and came up with what they referred to as "ideal" proportions. Human beings, ideally, were 7 heads tall. They also, through advanced study of mathematics and geometry, discovered a formula for perfect beauty. The golden ratio or golden mean. The formula is:

Width is to Length as Length is to Length + Width (w:l as l:l+w)

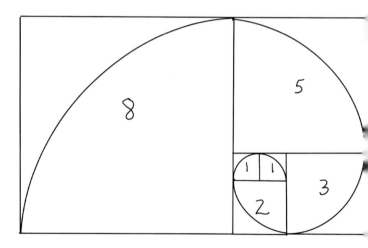

This ideal has been represented through paintings and sculpture throughout history, so that we can't know for certain that it is so pleasing because it is innate or because it is familiar. This ratio is found in many natural forms such as the nautilus shell, the human body, and many plant structures. The Golden Ratio is derived from the Fibonacci sequence discovered in approximately 200 BCE and named after an Italian mathematician in the 13th century, Leonardo of Pisa. When mapped out on a graph, the sequence creates a spiral that is consistently found in natural forms from sea shells to the entire universe.

This is a sequence of numbers in which each number is the sum of the two preceding numbers.

(0:1:1:2:3:5:8:13.....)

When a number in the sequence is divided by the preceding number, the ratio is 1:1.6, the Golden Ratio.

The same forms that exhibit the Golden Ratio also exhibit the Fibonacci sequence. Many art forms such as music (the scale is eight notes, a major chord is 1-3-5), poetry, painting, and sculpture use this ratio. It is still considered the most pleasing visual format.

What do we do with this information? We can use it in our designs as sizes for our elements. We can use it for overall dimensions of our compositions. Ideal sizes would be 48" x 78" or 36" x 58". I find these too long and thin for my taste.

MOVEMENT

Repetition, rhythm, and balance all are related to the design principle of "movement." Each of these is given an in-depth look in the following sections. Our eyes move across the surface elements of a composition in ways prescribed by the artist. Each type of movement creates a feeling or mood. Movement depends on placement of elements first and foremost. Of course, size, color, and texture of each unit also play into the sensation of movement, but arrangement is key. If the objects in the design are close together, the eye movement created is quicker. When spread out, the composition requires slower eye movement as it scans the surface.

Smaller components close together are quicker, large ones slower. Arrangement of color assists with movement but not necessarily the colors themselves. The colors can create a mood, which can be associated with movement. Lighter colors seem to be calmer and more peaceful and therefore are considered slower. Bright colors are much brisker and create a faster rhythm. Some elements can attract a lot of attention and give the eye a "pause" before continuing across the surface.

A bull's-eye in the center of a design is thought to be an eye stopper because it demands the viewer's immediate attention but can be used effectively to pull the viewer into the composition. If we consider a pattern as "texture," a strong print can promote movement if judiciously placed across the piece. The pattern will have its own rhythm, and it's important to take that into consideration when you decide to use one in your quilt. The quilt at top right is titled *John Prine*, and the lines are used to create the sense of his tunes. *Peppermint Twist* at bottom right swirls through the use of curved lines in the design and again through the quilting that leads our eyes in circles. In the quilt *Gique*, made of pastels (*opposite page, top left*), the sense of movement is slower both because of the color, but also because of the horizontal and vertical underlying structure.

John Prine

Peppermint Twist

Gique

Bubble

Untitled by Robin O'Neal

In the photo of the quilt *Bubble* (*top right*), featuring the printed fabrics by Anna Marie Horner and Michael Lunn, it is obvious how much rhythm and visual texture they create.

The movement created by the closely placed lines in the quilt by Robin O'Neal (*right*) is counterintuitive to the idea that horizontal lines are calm and peaceful. Through bright colors in the lines and tiny squares that cause our eye to dance across the surface, she has made this piece very happy and active. She has created a pattern through piecing.

UNITY/HARMONY

When a composition is unified, an agreement exists among the elements. They look like they belong together, that some visual connection has caused them to come together. Even though unity and harmony are often grouped together, I feel there's a subtle difference in the two terms. Unity is more objective. All the objects play nicely together. Harmony, though, implies a friendlier unity. The entities go together but go a step further and really sing!

Dance in Celery

The simplest way to achieve unity is with repetition—of color, of shape, of direction, of texture. Our eyes follow patterns and lines easily. Think of how we read. A quilt with a limited palette and similar shapes will always appear unified, as in the quilt *Dance in Celery* on the opposite page. In *Tattered History of Indigo* (*left*), though, all the shapes are different. Harmony is achieved through color and style. Also for this quilt, the repetition of quilting patterns and technique of raw edge appliqué unifies the design.

Below, *Corona Spring* is unified by a bright color palette even though the colors are all over the spectrum. What also ties this one together is the repetition of shapes and style. The decorative drawings over the surface pull the parts together even more. Curves and linear elements in different sizes make it work.

Tattered History of Indigo

Ways to create a sense of unity include similarity of shape, color, style, texture, and pattern. Repetition, rhythm, and arrangement play into how unified a design appears. When a composition is unified, the WHOLE predominates over the parts. Yes, there are parts that play major roles in the design, but you should see ALL first and foremost. The human brain is programmed to find patterns and harmony. This probably comes from prehistory, and the ability to spot an aberration was important for survival (that tiger among the trees).

To be successful, the composition should be unified and harmonious intellectually and visually. A design might have a strong message, but if it's too difficult to read because it is poorly organized, it just doesn't work. A composition that is beautiful but void of any meaning or suggestion is easily dismissed.

Corona Spring

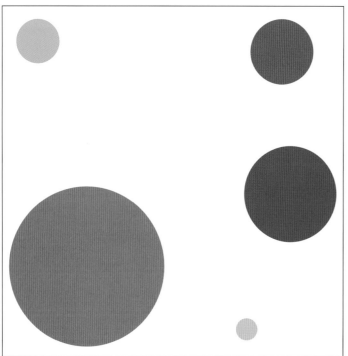

Grouping elements together or at least keeping them in proximity, is another strategy to develop unity. When items are close to each other, they create a conversation or pattern between them. There's a perfect distance that feels "sexy" or "right." A visual magnetic pull is created. Once that boundary is violated, the relationship breaks up and the objects feel disparate.

The circles on the left feel unified because of their proximity to one another, while the same-sized circles on the right, even though the same color, are too far apart to create a visual dialogue between them.

One way to establish a visual connection that is less obvious and allows objects to be spread farther apart is "directional" pull. Implied lines and points on objects create visual references for our eyes to move easily across a surface. In *Flamenco*, even though the left swirling curves could seem incongruous with the more severe black shape on the right, the curved lines both in the background and in the figures lead the eye around the surface of the composition. Not only do we intellectually understand the premise of the image, but it is unified through implied lines and movement.

Flamenco

These three quilts have always been problematic as to unity. I have tried for many years to find a way to combine more-realistic renderings with abstraction. I don't think the quilt to the left works. The purple "grapes" and the shaded pinkish area are not harmonious with the flat red and white shapes or the acid-green background. The same holds true with *Nascence*, the quilt at bottom right. The "eggs" seem out of place with the rest of the composition. The quilt at bottom left makes me happy, and I consider it unified. There aren't any shaded areas, but only large expanses of patterned fabrics to play with the flat decorative elements.

Spring Green

Flourish

Nascence

REPETITION

Repetition is an easy strategy to create unity and order in a composition. When an element is repeated over the surface, our eyes travel seamlessly from element to element. A grid is a tool employed by artists to organize objects in a design. This technique uses a framework on which to place the elements so that one visually leads to the next. In quilting, an arrangement of blocks is the obvious example of how this works. In *Linked*, the repetition of the dots, the black and white squares, the larger color squares, and even the vertical lines all create the visual unity. In the quilts on the facing page, the repetition of shapes and colors obviously creates visual unity. This is a simple strategy when designing a composition. If we draw a grid over the quilt, you can see that the grid does not have equally measured spacing, but it still organizes the elements effectively. The grid for *Send in the Clowns* is a regular grid often used for quilt designs. Repetition of color, shape, and texture also creates a pleasing unity in a design. Note the red "noses" in each block, and the repetition of black and white squares in the corners.

Linked

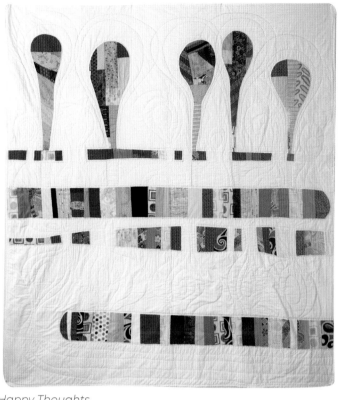

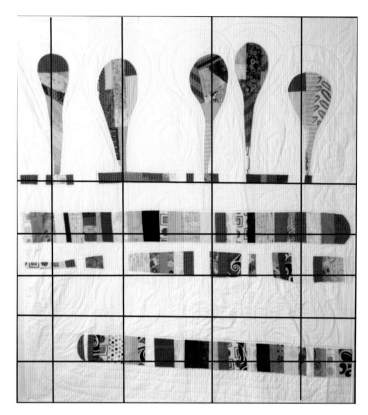

Happy Thoughts

Send in the Clowns

RHYTHM

Rhythm is closely related to repetition and movement. What differentiates it as a principle is that it is all about the pace of repetition or movement. Do the elements in a composition propel your eyes across the surface quickly or more slowly? Is it a slow, elegant waltz or a jazz swing? We often express rhythm in musical terms. The rhythms defined in music are legato, allegro, staccato. When our eyes move in a similar cadence in a design, a mood is created. Quick eye movements in a staccato rhythm create energy and excitement. A legato rhythm is smooth and flowing, therefore calm and relaxing. An allegretto is brisk and lyrical and is slower and smoother than the staccato. In *Rolling On*, the rhythm is clearly short-short-long, long-short-short along the horizontal direction. The rhythm is regular, following the vertical lines. Because of the way we read music, we often forget the vertical flow. Both directions are important in creating a design. The regularly spaced vertical tempo keeps this design organized and unified as it slows down the horizontal pace.

The rhythms of the top two quilts on the opposite page were created to depict dances. *Dancing with Belle* is a swirly waltz, and *Limbo* has a more staccato rhythm created with the placement of the lines. *Bobbing* is a large-scale quilt that flows as the viewer walks the length of it. The larger shapes and the horizontal line reinforce the effect.

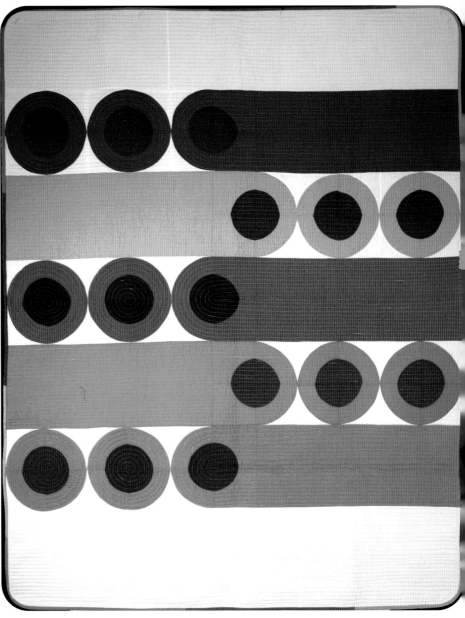

Rolling On

Dancing with Belle

Limbo

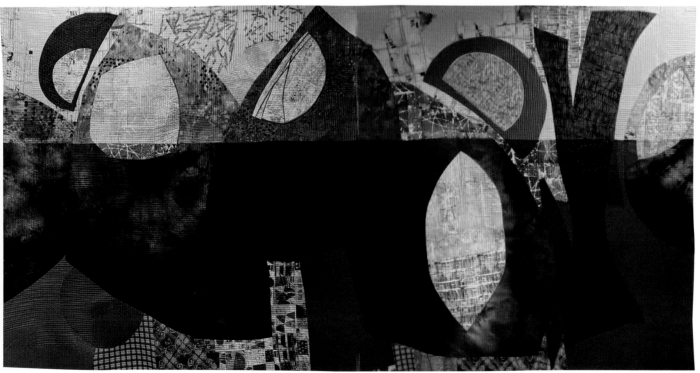

Bobbing

VARIETY

Variety is the spice of life. This is true in our food and in our designs. Whether highly spiced or mild in flavor, a composition without variety is just plain boring. Variety and unity need to work together to create an interesting but coherent composition.

We have already talked about creating interest through difference in shape, color, texture, and scale. It is clear that many of these design principles are similar, but with subtle differences. Movement across a design can be created by variety. Emphasis is necessarily created by difference. Rhythm is also dependent on variety, since different forms draw the eye in different tempos.

The element of value is one of the most important considerations to create variety. A design may have many colors and have diversity, but if they are all the same value, the surface becomes monotonous and muddy.

In a quilt that is block based or component based, diversity is important, even if subtle. An overall pattern is the nature of this type of design, and attention should be paid to variety of color and value to stave off boredom.

Matisse Study

I grew up in the kitchen above. Everything was brown. This monotonous color scheme didn't stop in the kitchen though. The bathrooms, the wood paneling, and the early American maple furniture all created a dull and uninspired environment. The remodel on the right created a fun space in which to prepare meals.

On the opposite page, the block-based quilt inspired by the drawings and prints of Matisse uses variety of color and value for interest, and the curves in the shapes create movement.

In the quilt at left, the design is leaning toward monotonous. Each block is exactly the same. The colors are all neutral and similar in value. Only the play of diagonals that creates the illusion of depth saves it from boredom.

Window Panes

To wrap this section up . . .

These are the elements and principles of design. They aren't rocket science. They are things you see every day as you look at television, your computer, billboards, and magazines. The best graphic designers in the world create all of those visuals. You KNOW them already. You FEEL the principles in your body as you balance on your feet or choose the color of your walls and your clothes. Great design is not as much about following a set of rules as it is about how you think and experience the world.

When I attended graduate school at the California Institute of Art, we didn't learn about HOW to make a piece of art. We didn't take classes about how to mix color or use a silkscreen to make a print. We didn't discuss the principles of design even once. Instead we read books by Roland Barthes, Michel Foucault, Gilles Deleuze, Jacques Derrida. We studied semiotics, the study of signs, that meaning is unstable, that to be human is to be informed by history. We talked about the viewer and the relationship between the artist and those who view the works and how that relationship is ever changing. We talked about how to THINK about making art, not about how to DO. It's about the conversation.

The courses in school were critiques and discussions that delved deep into the question "WHY?" Why did you use white? What does white mean to you? To others? The meanings of colors are different in different cultures. Why do you choose to quilt instead of paint? Why do you choose to hand-quilt instead of machine-quilt? How do each of these decisions inform what you are making? Each and every decision you make when you are creating is important to your final creation. Some of these decisions may seem very personal to you. Maybe you love a color because it was your grandmother's favorite color, and it reminds you of her. But even though personal to you, all decisions are universal. When others see your art, they bring their own personal experiences and preferences. The best art doesn't follow rules or present only a singular story. It is about universality and passion and investigation.

How do we do that? This is the essential question. We do that by being aware of WHY we make each decision. Awareness is at the heart of great art, not perfect technique. I am aware of many of the meanings of the color white when I am using white. I know what bright orange red can add to a composition because I know that red is about heat and heart and passion. As you can see, I use what I know about the element of design, color, and use it to bring a particular meaning.

In the next section, I want to talk about an essential part of the creative process—the art critique. It is through a discussion with other artists that we can learn to think about how we use the design principles to make better art and also how others see and experience our works. This process also helps you learn to express your "why." Until you need to articulate the different elements and principles you use, you may not think about the decisions you make as you create and whether or not they are working as you intend.

Fungi Dance by
Cheryl Thomson

CRITIQUE

WITHOUT GETTING ANGRY

WITHOUT GETTING HURT FEELINGS

WITHOUT GETTING A BIG HEAD

WITHOUT GETTING CONFUSED

AND

HOW TO USE THE EXPERIENCE TO HELP YOU GROW AS AN ARTIST

WHAT IS AN ART CRITIQUE?

My critique group was formed three years ago, and we have met almost every week since then. We have different skills and interests, but we also have equal passion for what we do. We all exhibit our work and have won awards. There is a respect and a friendship that creates a safe environment for us to talk about our work, the difficulties we are having, and the successes that happen, and to ask each other questions. What I love about our group is our inquisitive nature and, I have to say, our competitiveness.

Critique is a fundamental part of the artistic process, providing artists an opportunity to get a fresh pair of eyes on their artwork.

It is a TOOL to maybe see things in your work you hadn't previously seen. The viewpoints of others should be considered but not taken as a mandate to change what you are doing. YOUR voice is always the most important.

"CRITIQUE" has a connotation of "critical." Don't get caught up in the negative!

Instead, think of it as an analysis, evaluation, assessment, appraisal, appreciation, review, examination, or study.

There is always subjectivity involved in a critique. Not everyone agrees on everything. Nor should they. Every viewpoint is unique, based on many factors including experience, education, and level of expertise, to name a few. Remember that this is the purpose of a critique. You want as many viewpoints and opinions as you can get. This will enable you to see how others experience your artwork.

You don't want your critique partners to express only similar opinions to your own. You don't want to do critiques only with your good friends who love everything that you do. On the other hand, you don't want to do critiques with artists who are always overly critical or who are overly competitive. This is not a competition. It is a thoughtful discussion.

Choose critique partners whose work you admire. If you don't respect the work, you won't respect the comments. Your critique partners should be on a similar level of artistic exploration but don't need to have the same type of artistic practice.

It's important to remember that the WORK is NOT YOU! We all know this intellectually, but it's difficult to internalize. We all do some great work, and of course, we all do some that is not so good. The reason we are doing a critique is because we are asking for an honest and true opinion of what we are making. The information you get should help you make your work better; not make you feel good. If that is what you want, then post it online and wait for all the uncritical accolades! Prepare some questions prior to the critique. You might want to know if your color values are different enough to create a dramatic effect. Perhaps the lower right corner feels unresolved. You can ask if the elements don't play well with the rest of the artwork. Or maybe that element that you thought leads a viewer into the work might need to be adjusted because it's doing the opposite.

Take notes during your critique. Better yet, ask a friend to take notes about the discussion of your work, so that you can be present in the discussion instead of slowing down to write. You will be getting a lot of information, and you don't want to forget what was said. Take notes on the entire discussion. Many times, a comment relevant to another artist's piece might come in handy for your own work.

A critique should be a multifaceted, useful discussion between artists. You might have unintentionally created a line through your composition that cuts the piece in two. It's nice when someone asks if that was your intention, especially before you have sewn it all together. Be honest and thoughtful and kind. It is not a competition. It is a learning experience.

Image page 72: *Nascence*

When working on a piece in your studio, take a minute every day before you pick up your scissors or fabric to stop and take a good hard look at where you are in the process. Some evenings I think I have made major breakthroughs, only to discover the next morning that the light was different, and the colors don't work in daylight. Or I had a glass or two of wine and was suddenly a genius, only to discover, nope, I was very much disillusioned while under the influence. My best ideas come to me early in the morning, when I'm still a bit sleepy but my thoughts are clear. It's no mystery that our best ideas occur during these early hours or in the shower. Our brains are not cluttered with schedules or problems. We tend to "not think" while showering or waking, and we are open to new thoughts.

Some days, you might want to spend the entire afternoon performing a "critique" by yourself. When you stop and take the time to look, you will see things that may not have previously jumped out at you. Also, ask the question "Why?" to clarify your thoughts and process. We talk about spontaneity and intuition and the "spark," but the actual process is a slower assessment and in-depth study along the way.

Ask yourself, "Why did I choose these colors?" What do they mean to me and why am I drawn to them? Do they still serve me or are they merely comfortable? I know how they interact, and I don't have to think too hard to make them work for me. Colors have meaning, and are we using them to enhance our ideas or working at cross-purposes with our color choices?

Study the shapes you are using. Are you suddenly drawn to circles? Why? Maybe lines are the emphasis of your piece. Are the types of lines performing as you want them to? You might be making a composition about your experience at the beach. Are all your lines horizontal to depict the calmness of the sea? Was your visit to the beach only about relaxing? Maybe some diagonal or vertical lines will make the composition more interesting.

LET'S GIVE IT A TRY . . .

Study this quilt . . . it's one I love to use in my workshop because I think there are many questions that need to be asked.

Here are some of them:

What are those purple things, and are they doing what I want? Are they too different in style to work in this piece?

Is the green background effective or merely jarring?

What are the shapes in the lower left corner, and why do I keep them there? I do like them, but maybe they don't work.

Is the entire center area interesting or too different? What is the function of the painted fabric?

Is the entire piece a hot mess, or does it effectively express my feelings about spring and new growth?

Looking at it now, two years later, I realize that this may be more about how I feel about childbirth than an effective artwork. Childbirth is exciting, scary, human, warm, all-encompassing . . .

you get the idea.

The art is not great, but the concept is something I want to explore, and a fun discussion in a critique with other women!

Spring Green

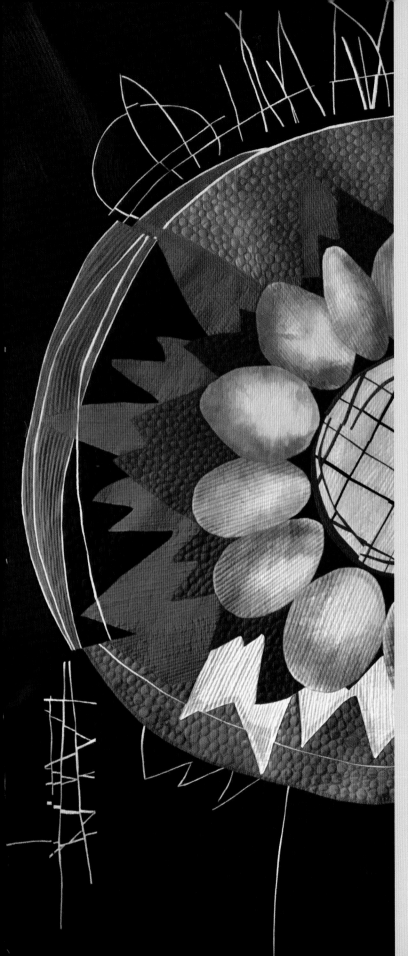

A CRITIQUE IS NOT . . .

. . . giving advice.
We want to talk about what we see, not how we would fix it or change it, even if asked for advice.

. . . the answer to how to "fix" something.
Everyone in the room will have a different opinion on how to move forward, and the only one that counts is the one that YOU, the artist, discover after a discussion of what might be working or not be working.

. . . free of confusion.
Many comments will contradict each other. It is YOUR, the artist's, mission to decide what to address and what not to.

. . . a blanket positive appraisal.
Some work is really, really good and we don't see anything to change. That is wonderful! But we don't want our statements to end up being just a thumbs up. Talk about what you see and why it "works" for you. Keep the discussion critical and not an Instagram heart.

THREE STEPS FOR A CRITIQUE:

1. DESCRIBE

2. ANALYZE

3. INTERPRET

1. Describe: What do you see?

Overall look

Does the piece look finished?

Is there "unity" in the piece? Does everything tie together well?

Does the composition work? Does it fit well together?

Does the whole piece "pop" off the wall—in a good way?

Where is your eye drawn to? Is that good or not so good for your design?

Do the values and colors provide depth and work together?

2. Analyze: Why do you see it?

Describe how the work is organized as a complete composition.

How is the work constructed or planned (movements, lines)?

Identify some of the similarities throughout the work (e.g., repetition of lines, shapes, color, movement).

Identify some of the points of emphasis in the work (e.g., subject, figure, movement).

If the work has subjects or characters or sections, what are the relationships between or among them?

3. Interpretation: How do you feel?

Describe how the work makes you think or feel.

Describe the expressive qualities you find in the work.

What expressive language would you use to describe the qualities (e.g., tragic, ugly, funny)?

Does the work remind you of other things you have experienced?

> NOTICE: It is not the opportunity to tell everyone what you see in the artwork. DO NOT say, "Oh! I see a horse—or a piano—or a boob!"
> Once you point something out, it can never be unseen!

ART ASSESSMENT SHEET

Overall Impression

Interesting?

Powerful?

Have variety?

Have unity?

Unique?

Have movement?

Have rhythm?

Balance/proportion

Does the composition feel lopsided or heavy in any area?

Does any element need to be repositioned to achieve balance?

Does an element feel too big? Or too small?

Is there an unintentional bull's-eye?

Do the colors balance?

Contrast

Is there size contrast?

Is there color contrast?

Is there value contrast?

Is there line/shape contrast?

Is there textural contrast?

Could additional contrast strengthen the piece? Where?

Color

Does any color strike you immediately as being wrong?

Do colors feel connected?

Would adding a color make the composition more interesting?

Would removing any color make the composition stronger?

Is there a clear sense of color relationships?

Are the color values creating a sense of depth?

Are your darks dark enough? Lights light enough?

Have you checked the values through gray scale?

Relationships

Are there coherent size relationships?

Are there coherent shape relationships?

Are there coherent textural relationships?

Do value relationships exist or make sense?

Do the stylistic relationships make sense?

Are thematic relationships supported by the combination of design and color elements?

Where could the relationships be strengthened?

Workmanship

Is the workmanship relevant to the work?

Are the techniques helping/hindering the overall design?

Do all the elements (techniques, quilting, binding) enhance the work? Or distract?

Magenta Trapunto

PUTTING IT ALL INTO PRACTICE

DESIGNING YOUR QUILT

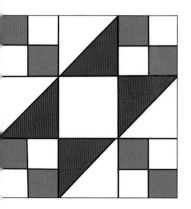
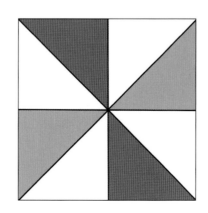
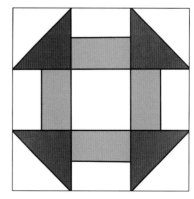

TECHNIQUES TO DESIGN A QUILT

There are many ways to design a quilt. When I started making quilts, I had no idea how many different techniques quilters use to make quilts. There are written patterns for specific designs. There are books and books of traditional block patterns from which to choose. Some of these block patterns are hundreds of years old, and I love the idea of making the same pattern made by a woman in the 1700s. During the Victorian era, crazy quilts made from silks and velvets with thousands of embroidery stitches were a necessity for a high-society sitting room. English paper piecing originated in the late 1700s and became one of the most popular quilt patterns in England. Trapunto and intricate whole-cloth quilting are early American quilt traditions brought from Europe. Quilts were made from old clothing, flour sacks, old blankets. Quilts were made to keep families warm, to show off stitching skills at county fairs, to mark and record special occasions, to beautify a home. What I love about quilting is that this history continues today.

In today's quilt world, you can use a pattern created by a quilt designer. Some quilt designers provide templates to make their patterns easier to use. Many pattern designers suggest fabrics for you, either using a new fabric line from a fabric-manufacturing company or examples to make the design look its best. If you choose this method, you know exactly how your quilt will look when it is finished. Or, you can be more adventurous and choose your own fabric and create a quilt that is unique to you. You can take the templates from a design and use them in a way that is different from the designer's instructions and discover new patterns. You can also make your own patterns. A popular way to design a quilt is by using a traditional quilt block and redesigning it. You can scale up the block so that one block becomes the entire design. It's fun to use different scales of the block in one quilt, to play across the surface together.

Paper piecing is another popular method for making a quilt. One method is foundation paper piecing, in which a paper template is used to stabilize the fabrics.

Tribute to Kathryn

Clandestine

Kaleidoscope

The fabric is sewn directly onto the paper, and then the paper is removed. Normally, intricate designs that require precision are paper pieced.

English paper piecing is also common. Fabric is wrapped around a cardboard template, then glued in place, and the pieces are hand-sewn together. Once the quilt is constructed, the templates are removed. How about designing a contemporary quilt entirely improvisationally? The definition of "improv" is "without a pattern." There are many ways to improv with fabric. One method is to cut fabric into small strips and squares (or grab scrap fabric pieces) and randomly pull one at a time out of a paper bag and sew them together spontaneously to create an overall dense pattern. Larger pieces of fabric can be cut into shapes and arranged into a design that will have more structure.

I have started cutting out large-scale shapes and designing directly on my design wall. I use black templates and then add color as I build the quilt.

And then there's drawing in a sketchbook or on a tablet, doodling, or being inspired by photographs and other forms of art. These drawings are the underlying designs for a quilt.

Let's look at each method more closely.

USING A PATTERN

Patterns for quilts have been around since the beginning of quilting for every kind of quilt, from highly complex appliqué quilts to whole cloth quilts. Patterns for every style from traditional to modern, even improv-type prompts for quilters to follow. Quilt magazines are full of patterns. There are books bursting with patterns. Many young quilters are earning a living by creating quilt patterns and selling them on their websites and through fabric stores.

Naive Melody pattern
by Lucy Engels

There are many different kinds of marking implements for use on fabric: chalk markers, water-erasable markers, pens that disappear with heat, hera markers, and ceramic markers. They all work for marking, but use chalk for best erasure and inks for lines that won't show on the front.

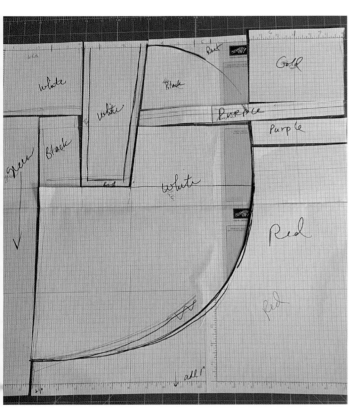

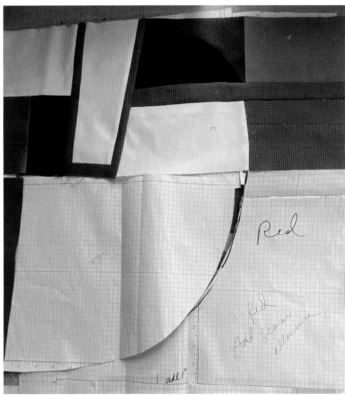

For this quilt, I drew my own pattern on graph paper the exact size I wanted it. I then cut out the pattern and added ¼" seam allowance around each when I cut out of fabric. Notice I labeled the colors so I wouldn't get confused!

USING TEMPLATES

Many quilt designers provide templates to use to make their patterns successfully. These templates are from Jenny Haynes. Her designs use a technique invented by Jenny to make perfect curves. I love that her sets of circles and ovals contain several different sizes of templates to make amazing patterns.

Ninja (detail)

Quilt by Jenny Haynes

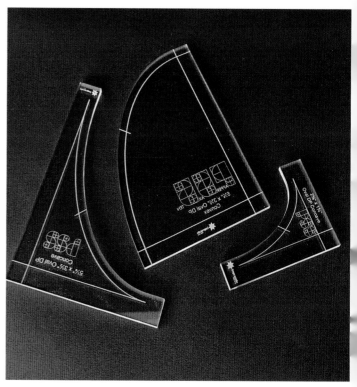

Templates designed by Jenny Haynes

PAPER PIECING

Paper piecing, or foundation paper piecing, is a technique useful for piecing complex designs and for precision piecing. The outline of the design is printed on a piece of paper. It became popular in England in the 1700s and was used to stabilize pieces of fabric to be stitched together. In the Victorian era, crazy quilts were all the rage, and the same technique was used on a base of muslin. These days, typing paper, freezer paper, and tracing paper are used. The fabric is sewn onto the backside of the paper, and when the block is complete, the paper is removed.

Ode to Rembrandt (detail)

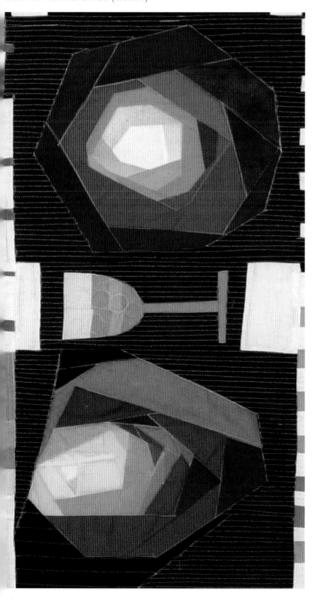

ENGLISH PAPER PIECING

English paper piecing, better known as EPP, has been around since the late 1700s. Fabric is wrapped around a cardboard shape, often glued in place and then hand-sewn to another shaped piece. Hexagons are most commonly used and are referred to as "hexies." The sewing is entirely by hand. Once all the shapes are sewn together, the cardboard is removed. One trick I learned is to punch a hole through the center of the cardboard shape before sewing. It makes removal much easier! Later in the book I give step-by-step instructions.

Kaleidoscope (detail)

Reverse appliqué is a technique used in molas, textiles created by the Kuna people in Panama. They are handmade using a reverse appliqué technique. Several layers (usually two to seven) of different-colored cloth (usually cotton) are sewn together; the design is then formed by cutting away parts of each layer. The edges of the layers are then turned under and sewn down.

Antique mola from Panama

APPLIQUÉ AND REVERSE APPLIQUÉ

Appliqué is a technique in which small pieces of fabric are cut out and then sewn or stuck onto a larger piece of fabric to create a pattern or picture. These "patches" of fabric can be attached onto another piece of fabric in several different ways. My favorite is the traditional method called "needle-turned appliqué," in which the edges of the patch are turned under using a needle and blind-stitched in place. I love the finished look of needle-turn. It creates a neat edge, and the appliqué sits up off the base fabric.

Raw-edge appliqué normally employs the use of a fusible interfacing that has heat-activated adhesive on either one side or both sides. Interfacings come in various thicknesses. Some are strings of glue formed into a sheet. Others are thicker and sewn onto delicate or unstable fabrics to give reinforcement as well as adhesion. I like to use them with silks and shot cottons to keep them from fraying so badly. As the name implies, the appliqué is either hand- or machine-sewn onto the base fabric with a zigzag or hem stitch. Some quilters like to use a straight stitch close to the edge or more-decorative stitches.

Tattered History of Indigo

TRAPUNTO (ITALIAN) AND BOUTIS (FRENCH)

Stuffed quilting, or trapunto, was known in Sicily as early as the 13th century. The word "trapunto" means "to quilt" in Italian. In the "real" trapunto method, a quilt is quilted, then sections to be "poufed" are slit and extra padding is inserted. The slit is then closed with fine stitching.

Boutis is also a form of "stuffed" quilting, but the technique is different. Yarn is pulled through a layer of fine cotton that has been stitched together in a design by hand or machine. The yarn is pulled through the shapes one strand at a time and then clipped off. The ends are then maneuvered back into the shape. A boutis quilt is only two layers of fine cotton; the only "batting" is the yarn in each shape.

The method we most use now is as follows:

1. Draw or trace a pattern onto fabric with a fabric pen.

2. Center fabric over high-loft batting (1/2"–1") and pin into place with safety pins, basting stitches, or straight pins.

3. Stitch along perimeter of design elements (follow the pattern lines) with water-soluble thread.

4. Cut away batting to the stitched perimeter with small, sharp scissors.

5. Layer the quilt top with batting attached to a second layer of batting (lower loft) and the quilt back.

6. Quilt as desired.

7. Gently soak in warm water to dissolve water-soluble thread leaving only the final quilting thread.

Design being transferred onto fabric with a fabric pen. Don't use the disappearing-in-air pens because they might disappear before you want them to!

Below: High-loft batting stitched onto fabric and cut away. Images from front and back. Below you can see the finished quilted pieces. Hand or machine quilting works very nicely.

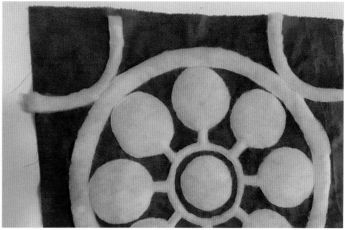

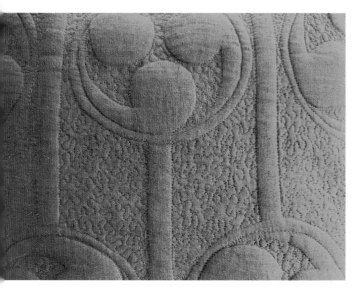

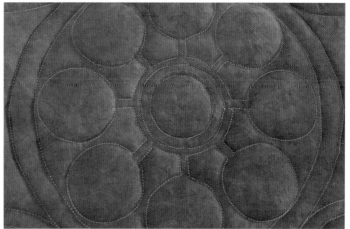

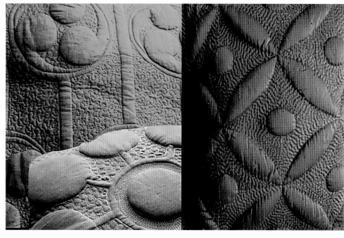

IMPROVISATION

My favorite way to design a quilt is to play with fabric on my design wall and create a piece that is entirely improvisational. Because I am a painter by training and have years of art practice, this method suits my temperament and feeds my creativity in ways that I can't get by following a pattern. "Improvisation" is defined as "not using a pattern." That's it.

There are so many ways to improv and so many talented instructors for improv that it's not easy to give a comprehensive listing. Some instructors concentrate on improv curves. Some on strip piecing. Some begin with an inspiration photo or idea. Mine begins without any preconceptions and builds entirely intuitively on a design wall. I teach "Dancing with the Wall," a method of improv in which the design starts in the center with a single element and grows one piece at a time until the quilt is designed. The components are then pieced together. My method stresses observation of each step and then responding to the design that is on the wall at each step.

More recently, I've started designing quilts by placing very large shapes on the design wall and improv-ing off them. Is this technically improv? It's not really a pattern per se, but there is more forethought than starting from scratch. The improvisation comes with choices of color and additional elements as the quilt designs grow. I like to work figure and ground simultaneously, concentrating on balance of color and scale.

There are many new fabric designers using original artwork to create fabrics that sing with color and pattern. I use them in large pieces to showcase the pattern as much as I can. In this piece, I laid out all the fabric (Lunn Fabrics, eBond, Kaffe Fassett, Tim Holtz) and based the entire composition on the strength of the patterns.

Waiting In Line
at SXSW

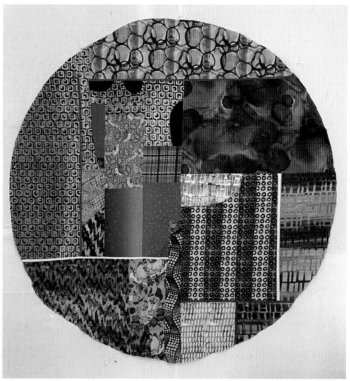

Bubble

This quilt started with strips of hand-dyed fabric and quadrants of curves that began to form a "head." Almost all the fabric in this quilt was hand-dyed, and it gives a nice soft overall color. Pops were added through commercial fabrics in strips and partial circles. Note that the empty spaces across the top are scraps from my bin, arranged to complement the rest of the quilt.

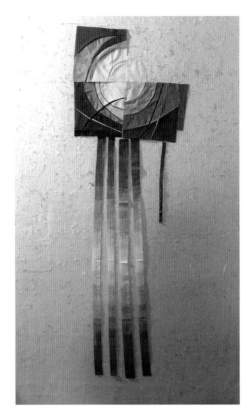

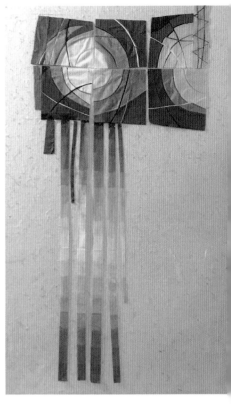

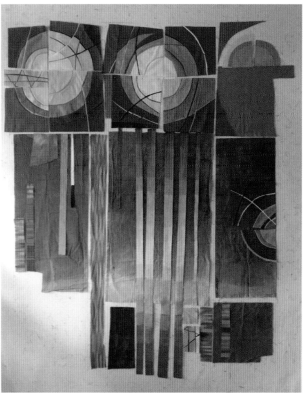

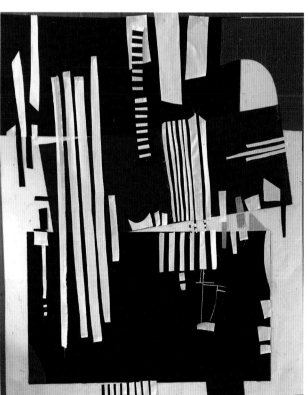

In *Bonnie Raitt*, I started with three large slabs of black and started improving on top of them with strips of white. I kept adding elements, including the red scrap in the top right corner. I felt as if more detail would add interest, and added the thin line elements last.

Untitled by Ruth Mendel

Practice of Kovarik-style stitching by the author

Stitching can also be improvisational. In the quilt above, Ruth Mendel created an additional layer of meaning with her stitching in a workshop taught by Paula Kovarik. On the right, I was practicing stitching Paula Kovarik–style stitching.

For those of you who don't know, Paula Kovarik is the master of improv stitching, and her book *At Play In the Garden of Stitch* is highly reccommended for instruction and inspiration. She machine-stitches and hand-stitches in combination to create her inventive quilts, which are full of humor and intelligence. She is also an improv piecer and appliquér. Believe it or not, Kovarik cuts her award-winning quilts into pieces and rearranges them or constructs three-dimensional masks and critters from them!

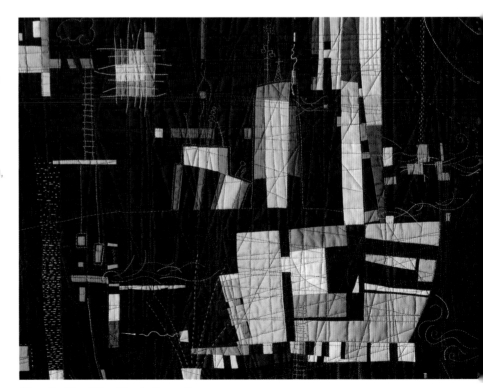

Signals (detail) by Paula Kovarik

Unglued (detail) by Paula Kovarik

DESIGNING/DRAWING WITH ART, APPS & PHOTOGRAPHY

Drawing and painting apps have become very common and are available for cell phones, tablets and iPads, laptop computers, and desktop computers. Many are free. Most that aren't free are very reasonably priced. These apps are powerful little pieces of software and can be used for simple sketches as well as complex masterpieces. On these two pages I have used photographs and a drawing as the inspiration for these quilts.

Original photograph

Black Spring

Original photograph

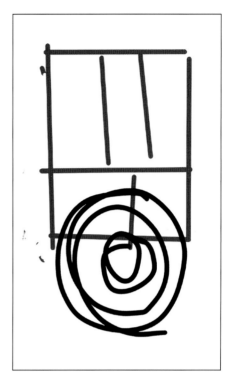

Illustration using Procreate

Bloom

Black over Red

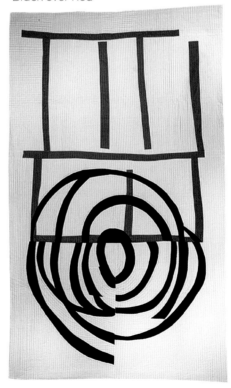

ENGINEERING

Now that you have designed your quilt, you will next decide how to actually construct it.

You can sew it all together by hand. Quilts have been constructed by hand sewing for thousands of years.

Or use a sewing machine to piece your quilt.

If it's an appliqué quilt, either of these methods can be used. There's hand-stitched needle-turn appliqué. There's raw-edge machine appliqué. Pieces of fabric can be glued onto another piece of fabric with fusible interfacing and then stitched on a machine. Zigzag and blanket stitches are the most-common stitches to use, but the more decorative stitches that come with most sewing machines can add interest.

Design elements such as fabric yo-yos and couching and prairie points can be applied to the quilt top. Rick-rack, cording, beads, buttons, embellishments, ribbons, embroidery, paint, drawings—just about anything can be put on a quilt!

How do you decide how to engineer your quilt?
I love to piece. I love the puzzle of it. I have used appliqué on

a few quilts, but I love the look and the challenge of actually piecing it by machine. The decision of what method to use to engineer your quilt is based not only on the aesthetic you prefer, but also your skill level and the type of quilt you are making.

Many "art" quilts, particularly those that are pictoral, use raw-edge appliqué. You can see in the fun quilt by Lin Elmo (*bottom left*) that many tiny pieces of fabrics are used to make the image, and they would be impossible to piece!

In the quilt by Ruth Mendel, *Stone Spiral*, she combines techniques by hand appliquéing the stones onto a pieced ground. The small oval shapes would be difficult, if not impossible, to inset or piece into the background and leave the carefully constructed piecework intact.

Each quilt has a personality, and it's up to you to decide how best to sew it all together. If you are new to piecing and have intricate shapes, then it's okay to appliqué them on top. If you love the challenges of piecing, there are many techniques to make it easier.

by Lin Elmo

Stone Spiral by Ruth Mendel

METHODS AND INSTRUCTIONS FOR ENGINEERING

HAND SEWING
PIECING BY MACHINE
APPLIQUÉ/COLLAGE

Each method of putting your quilt together has many variations. There are, of course, hundreds of tutorials on the Internet for each method. In the next few pages, I am going to show you the way I was taught or have found to work best for me. I learned to hand-piece from Tara Faughnan, and I love her method. I learned to machine-piece in a beginner's workshop at a local quilt store. My favorite way to appliqué is from a tutorial by Carol Friedlander on her website. I encourage you to experiment with various techniques and find what works best for you.

Hand sewing can be used for any quilt construction technique from paper piecing to appliqué. Before sewing machines were invented, all quilts were hand-sewn! I love the softness and texture of a hand-pieced quilt but don't have the patience to make one very often. On the opposite page, the pieces are cut out using a template and arranged on the design wall. The arcs are pieced first, then the "melons" are sewn on, and finally the centers are attached to make blocks. The blocks are then sewn together into larger sections.

Machine piecing is self-explanatory. The fabrics are sewn together on a sewing machine. Machine piecing can be simple or very complex, depending on the type of quilt you are making and whether or not you are using a pattern. Many times when using a pattern and many of the same elements such as half-square triangles, chain piecing is a fast method for machine sewing. Traditional blocks are often chain-pieced because all the blocks contain the same pieces but may differ in color or orientation.

Improv quilts may be more challenging to piece because they are not predesigned and don't normally include seam allowance. These "petals" are machine-pieced. You can see that I split them in half in order to make them easier to piece. Tight curves love to pucker and never lie flat, so I just cut them in two! I like that they don't line back up!

Sewing your components together can look daunting, but don't panic! You can do it! First, take a photograph of your quilt and study

it carefully. Identify the longer seams to divide the piece into sections. Draw lines on the photo to help you do this.

When you have divided the picture of your piece into sections, start construction by sewing small components into larger components. Find adjoined pieces that are similar in size or easily sewn together, and sew those first. As you work, starch and press each seam well. You will find it easier to work with stiffer pieces. Floppy fabric that hasn't been starched stretches more and is more difficult to control. If you are working with a component with a bias edge, starch extra well and press, don't iron, because it can quickly be ironed out of shape.

This is the time to square off each section as you go. You might need to straighten some components by cutting off diagonal edges or to even up seam edges. Don't worry; this won't affect your overall design. In some places, you will need to add more fabric to make a component a little larger, and sometimes you might need to trim a piece to fit. I almost always add fabric to a piece instead of trimming its partner piece. I'd rather have more fabric to work with than perhaps cut something too small. If you do trim, be careful when you trim not to affect the component negatively. As an example, if you are needing to cut down a checkerboard, the trimmed-off row will become a row of rectangles instead of squares.

It sometimes helps to use tracing paper to assist in piecing wonky sections. I trace the section while it's on the design wall. I then take the tracing to the cutting table and place the components on top of it. I find that isolating and laying a section out flat helps with visualizing how to put it together. If you need to add fabric, it is nice to be able to make a pattern from the tracing so that you make the added piece the correct shape and size.

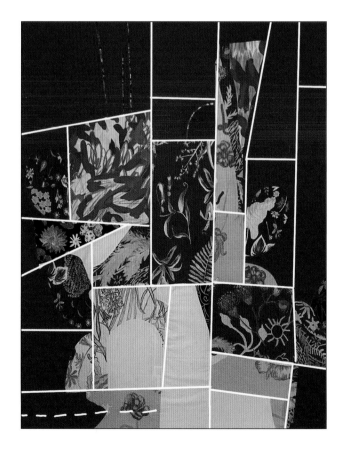

HOW TO HAND-PIECE

1. Make a template from cardboard or plastic without $1/4$" seam allowance. (1)
2. Trace onto fabric. Cut out, adding $1/4$" seam allowance. Mark intersections of lines. (2)
3. Sew seam with tiny running stitches, starting and stopping at marks. DO NOT sew all the way to the edge. (3a, 3b, 3c)

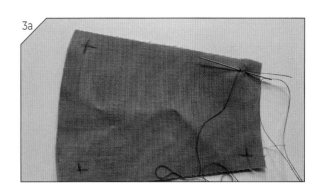

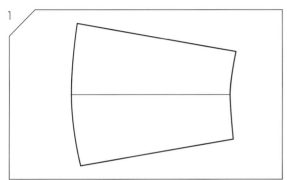

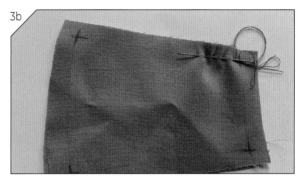

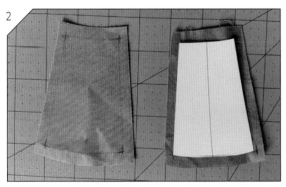

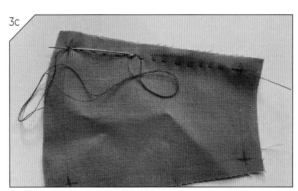

HERE ARE SOME OF THE COMMON CHALLENGES YOU MAY FACE . . .

PARTIAL SEAMS

Partial seams are two seams that don't line up. You will need to sew one seam partway, stop, and sew the other seam, and then go back and finish the first one. Remember, you want to sew the longest seam last.

Y-SEAMS

Y-seams are actually seams that come together in a "Y" and are handled differently than partial seams. With Y-seams, you will sew your seam and stop short $1/4$" of the final seam. Then, with the needle down, turn your piece and line up the other seam. Finish sewing.

ABSOLUTELY IMPOSSIBLE

There are some sections that are absolutely, definitely, no-question impossible to engineer. When you realize you have created these types of sections, you have a couple of options. One option can be to choose an alternate piecing method, usually appliqué. Another option is to modify your design so that it becomes possible. I have had to modify many sections of quilts and realize that these little "tweaks" do not make a huge difference in the appearance of my overall quilt.

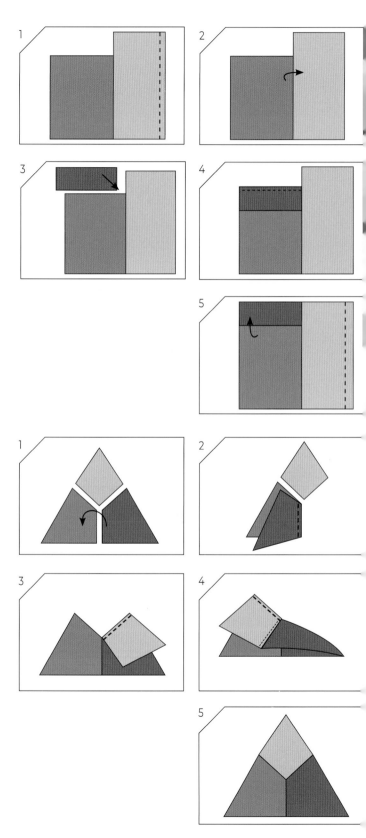

½" VS. ¼" EXTRA FOR INSERTING SHAPES . . . WHICH DO YOU USE WHEN? HERE'S THE LOWDOWN . . .

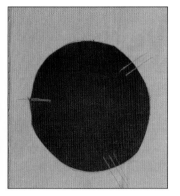 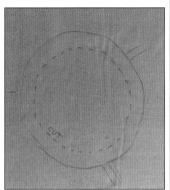

If you are inserting a shape into a background, draw around your shape. In three or four places, draw registration lines on both pieces. Remove your shape and measure ½" inside your drawn line. Cut on that line. This is confusing because we need only a ¼" seam allowance, right? No, we need to add the seam allowance for both the background and the shape together, making the measurement ½". Yes, the drawn line will show after the shape is inserted. It's a good idea to use a good disappearing fabric marker.

If you are not entirely inserting a shape, but sneaking it into the edge of the background, then ¼" is fine if you scootch the shape ¼" off the edge. This is the seam allowance, and the edges of the ground and shape will meet up.

If you don't scootch the shape off the edge, the edges will not line up after it is sewn in because there is no seam allowance added to either the ground or the shape.

HOW TO MAKE EIGHT HALF-SQUARE TRIANGLES AT ONCE:

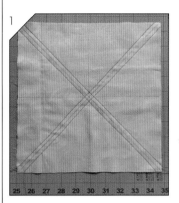 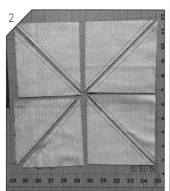

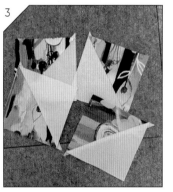 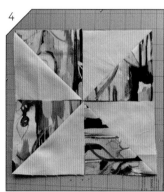

If you are needing many half-square triangles for a pattern, this method makes eight at a time. Cut a square from two fabrics and layer them with right sides together. Draw diagonal lines from corner to corner through the center and sew ¼" on both sides of each line. Draw vertical and horizontal lines. Cut the squares apart on the drawn lines. Open and press well.

The formula for making your half-square triangles the correct size:

finished half-square triangle size + ⅞" (.875) x 2

4" finished square + ⅞" = 4.875 x 2 = 9.75"

HOW TO PIECE IMPROV CURVES ON A MACHINE:

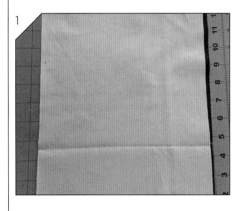

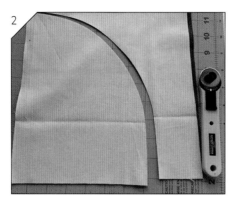

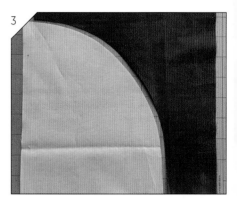

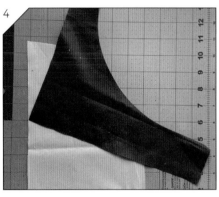

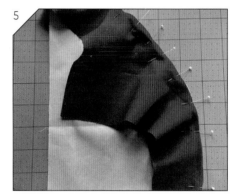

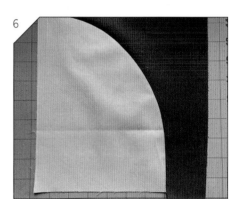

1. Place two fabrics together right sides up. (1)

2. Cut curve through both fabrics. (2)

3. Using one of each color, pin together, beginning in the center and working toward each end. The ends will not line up because there is no seam allowance. (3, 4, 5)

4. Sew with concave side up to help prevent puckers. (6)

5. Press open and trim. (7)

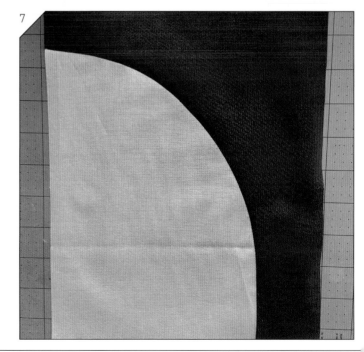

HOW TO DO FOUNDATION PAPER PIECING

To begin a paper-pieced quilt, print out the pattern on copy paper, freezer paper, or commercial paper made for paper piecing. Notice that the finished paper-pieced block is reversed from the pattern. The fabric is placed onto the back of the paper but sewn from the front. If it sounds confusing, I think it is! It always takes me a couple of seams to get it straight in my head.

One tendency to avoid is to cut your fabric pieces too small. Our eyes deceive us as to the size we need to fill the space we are working on. Some paper piecers swear by their $1/4$" special paper-piecing ruler tool that is available.

There are two methods to paper-piece. One is with a pattern such as the one shown here, which is sewn into a block and then all the paper torn out. There is also a method done with freezer paper in which the paper pattern remains intact. In this method, the freezer paper is turned back and the seam is sewn only through the fabric.

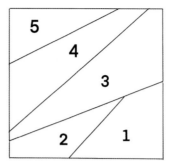
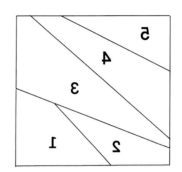

1. Print paper patterns on copy machine. Cut out each pattern, adding $1/4$" all the way around, which will act as the seam allowance when the blocks are sewn together to construct the quilt. Fold on all lines and, if you want, stitch without thread to perforate the lines. This will make the paper easier to remove when you are all done. Place first fabric behind pattern. From this side, it will be wrong side up.

2. Fold back pattern and trim fabric, adding $1/4$" seam allowance. Remember, from front of pattern it's wrong side up. This is where I always get confused. You don't need to sew this first piece, but position it in place (a spot of glue helps).

3. Line up second fabric with first and sew on the line from the front.

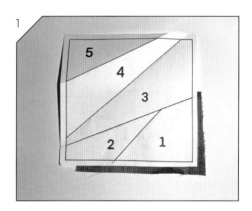
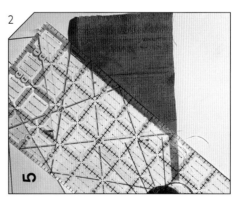

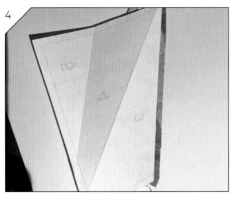

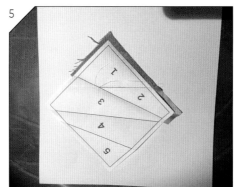

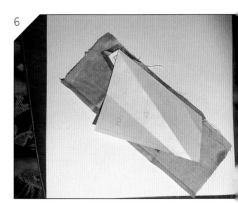

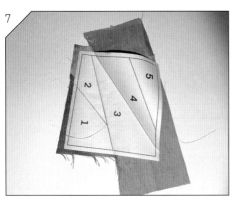

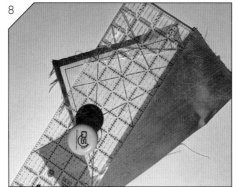

4. Fold paper back and trim to $1/4$".

5. The open up and press seam from back.

6. Line up next fabric, making certain it is large enough to cover its designated area. Open pattern and sew on line from front.

7. Open fabric and press well from back.

8. Fold back next pattern line and trim fabric to $1/4$".

9. View of stitching on the line.

10. Completed block from front.

HOW TO DO ENGLISH PAPER PIECING

EPP uses paper templates covered by fabric. Shapes for templates can be squares, equilateral triangles, or hexagons. Hexies are the most popular shape, but play with other shapes for distinctive patterns!

SUPPLIES FOR EPP

- fabrics
- cardstock templates (purchased or homemade)
- water-based glue stick
- scissors
- 50–80 wt thread
- size 11–12 sharp needle

---

1. Cut shapes from fabric, adding ¼" seam allowance on all sides.

2. Place template in center of fabric.

3. Using a water-based glue stick, dot glue on all edges of fabric.

4. Fold over all seam allowances tightly against edges of template.

5. All edges glued in place. Use glue sparingly—a dot will do. Otherwise, it's difficult to remove template.

6. Gather thread (50 wt or smaller gauge) and needle. A sharp size 11 or 12 works best.

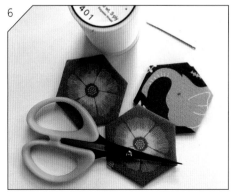

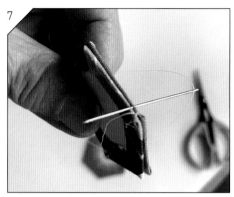

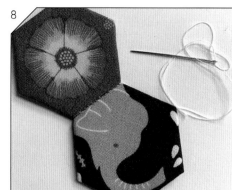

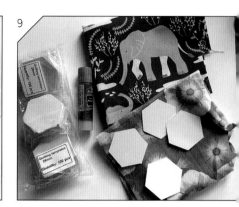

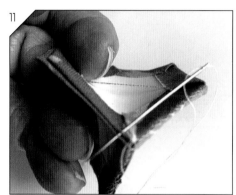

7. Whipstitch the edges of two pieces, catching a couple of threads only. Make stitches small.

8. Two hexies sewn together from front.

9. Add another hexie and join it with whipstitch.

10. Stitch to other side of center hexie.

11. Remove templates. To make this step easier, punch a hole in the center of each template before you start.

12. And first three done! Keep working around center. Add as many rows as you desire.

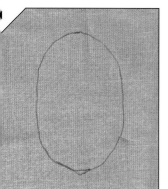 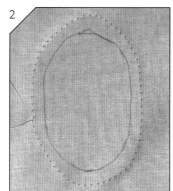 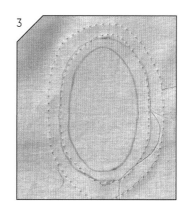 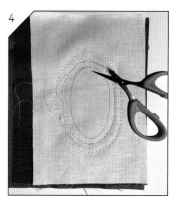

REVERSE APPLIQUÉ

1. Stack two or more fabrics right sides up and mark shape on the top one about ¹/₄" smaller.

2. Stitch by hand or machine ¹/₄" outside of circle.

3. I drew an inner circle for the third color for placement.

 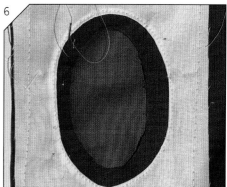

4. Being careful to cut through only top fabric, cut out shape.

5. Clip any curves or corners to make turning under of fabric edges easier and smoother. Turn edges under. Press well. Hand- or machine-stitch.

6. If more layers, cut out next shape at least ¹/₄" inside of last.

7. Turn edges under. Press well and hand- or machine-stitch. If you stack more fabrics, keep cutting and stitching in this manner until all the layers have been exposed. I used white thread to stitch, but to make your stitches disappear, match threads to each layer.

NEEDLE-TURNED APPLIQUÉ

Needle-turned appliqué is just what it says. Cut out a shape and, with large running stitches, baste it in place about $\frac{1}{4}$" from the raw edge. Using a thin needle and thread that matches the appliqué fabric, stitch the appliqué to the background. The stitches should be close together, and the needle should barely touch the turned edge. Use the point of the needle to turn the edges of the fabric under as you sew. Turn under only about $\frac{1}{8}$" as you go, and use your fingernails to hold it in place. As you can see, I'm a lousy appliqué stitcher! But look at the fine work of Chris Fornell and Patti Coppock!

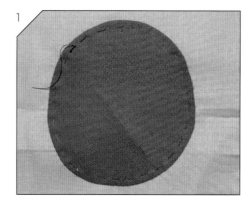

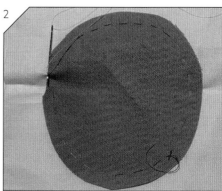

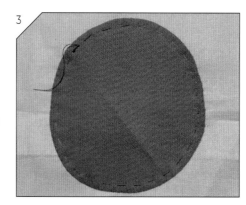

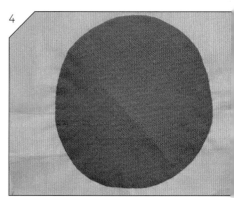

Right: *So What Did You Eat Today?* by Patti Coppock and Chris Fornell. Above: Detail.

A fairly recent product, dissolvable interfacing, has made appliqué easier for all of us appliqué-challenged. The appliqué shape is cut from the interfacing, which can either be heat-set or sticky-backed, and attached to the fabric. Cut $1/4$" larger than the interfacing shape and neatly turn under the edges and stitch onto the base fabric. The interfacing may be dissolved in warm water or left in as you desire.

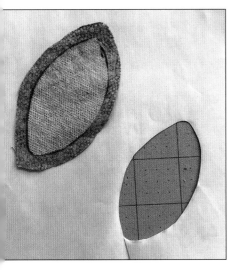

APPLIQUÉ CIRCLES

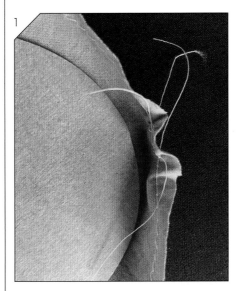

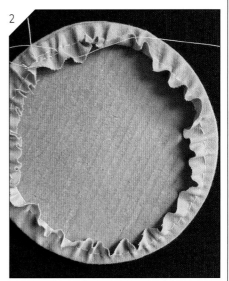

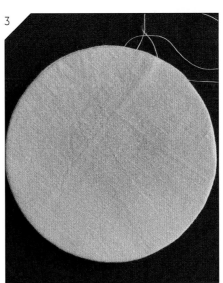

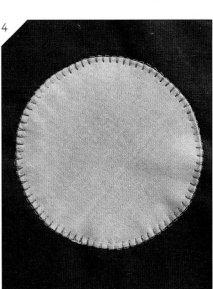

One way to create perfect appliqué circles or ovals is to use a template. In this illustration, I made a cardboard circle. Cut a fabric circle at least $1/2$" larger than the template. By hand or using a large machine stitch, sew $3/16$" in from the edge of the fabric circle. Pull bobbin threads, both at the same time, to gather the fabric around the cardboard circle, keeping it as centered as you can. When the fabric is tightly encased, use starch and press the edges. Remove the cardboard and re-press. Appliqué by hand or machine. Voilà!

QUILTING

Your quilt is all sewn into one beautiful, flat flimsy. Now you need to decide how to quilt it. I find this the most challenging part of a quilt, mostly because I am not good at it.

A quilt is made of three layers sandwiched together. The pieced top, or flimsy, the batting/wadding/felt, and the back. This quilt sandwich is stitched together either by hand sewing, tying, or machine sewing. Some quilters make fun backs for their quilts. Some use wide-backing fabrics (108" wide). When I had the opportunity to be a "white-glove" volunteer for a quilt exhibition, I discovered very special backings and was delighted to show off the backs as well as the fronts of quilts.

The type of batting to use is another decision that determines the final appearance of your quilt. Battings come in different "lofts" or thicknesses and are also made from different materials. Wool, cotton, polyester, bamboo, and silk are the most-common types, many in combination. All battings these days have great drape and are easy to sew through. Polyester battings are available in bright white and also black, but they are warmer. Using a high-loft batting such as wool or even cotton/wool makes a puffy, soft quilt. It's counterintuitive, but wool batting is preferred for warm climates because it is more breathable. If you don't want any puff, you can use wool or polyester felt. This is normally reserved for quilts that will hang on the wall, because they aren't very drapable or soft. Battings also have suggestions for the widest distance you can leave unquilted and the quilt will still hold together through use. Fusible batting is also available from several companies. These are good for smaller projects.

Hand quilting is one choice. As we've seen, hand quilting has a soft, distinguishable texture. In the days of quilting bees, a quilt was stretched onto a large wooden frame, and many quilters sat around the frame quilting. I hear tales of eight to

ten stitches to the inch being the norm. So tiny. Something to strive for that takes hours of practice. Quilting bees aren't common today, and the quilting is done by an individual. Large hoops are available in circles or ovals for stretching a quilt in sections for ease. Many quilters don't use a hoop at all. All three layers of the quilt should be basted together with long stitches to hold everything in place. Safety pins can be used for machine quilting but are difficult when hand quilting with a hoop.

Machine quilting has become the most popular quilting method with the arrival of longarm quilting machines. Even though expensive (ranging from a few thousand dollars to over $30k), these large industrial machines are efficient and provide opportunities for fun quilting patterns. They can be used with or without a computer to predetermine quilting patterns. Many machines also have the "pantograph" feature, in which a paper pattern is positioned on the back of the machine and lines are followed with a laser beam. These are

Cotton Batting	$1/8$"–$1/4$" loft	Durable, soft	quilt up to 8" apart
Wool Batting	$1/3$"–$1/2$" loft	Lightweight, soft	quilt up to 8" apart
Polyester Batting	$1/8$"–$1/2$" loft	Durable, low crease	quilt up to 10" apart
Bamboo/Silk	$1/8$"–$1/4$" loft	Environmental	quilt up to 8" apart
Green (recycled materials)	$1/8$"–$1/4$" loft	Environmental	quilt up to 10" apart

usually edge-to-edge patterns and allow even beginning quilters the opportunity to include fun stitching motifs. Longarm machines are normally mounted on a frame and take up a lot of real estate. The quilting is done by moving the needle, driven by handles, over the surface of the quilt.

Longarm machines are also available as "sit-down" machines. On this type of machine, the quilt is moved under the needle and can be quilted using "free motion," in which the quilter creates the quilting pattern on the surface. Rulers are available in many shapes and sizes as well to use as guides for quilting (rulers can also be used on frame-mounted longarm machines).

Our domestic sewing machines can also be used for quilting. Smaller quilts are more fun and more easily quilted on a domestic. Companies are making machines with wider "throats" to facilitate quilting, which are much less expensive than a "longarm," whose necks are 16" or greater. Some of the newer machines have 30" necks for greater versatility in quilting patterning. On a domestic machine, the quilt is rolled and placed over your shoulder and fed through the machine. It is very important to have your quilt sandwich well-basted or pinned for ease of manipulating the quilt as you go.

Because of the expense of longarm machines, quilters are going into the quilting business. They offer the public quilting services from pantographs to computerized to specialty patterns at prices much more reasonable than buying a machine. When hiring a longarmer, do your research. References from other quilters are invaluable. You will be working closely with your quilter, and it's important that you have a rapport, and that they are willing to work closely so that you know what you are getting. Ask for samples of their quilting and types of quilting they are comfortable performing. I know very talented quilters who can quilt anything! I also know quilters who prefer computerized patterns so that they have more time to work on their own quilt projects.

DIFFERENT QUILTING PATTERNS CREATE DIFFERENT EFFECTS!

On the next pages, I took a contemporary design and made six identical pieced panels. I then sent them off to my really talented quilting good friend Mandy Ruden and asked her to create six quilting patterns to see how each affected the overall look of the finished piece. I am often surprised at how a quilting pattern can completely change the look of a design. She chose to quilt a "simple" version and a "complex" version of each type of design.

1. In the first two, she used straight vertical lines. The first panel is quilted with lines 1" apart. The second panel is matchstick-quilted, $\frac{1}{8}$" apart. The 1" quilted pattern creates a soft, fluffy appearance as well as a soft, fluffy tactility. If you are wanting a quilt to put on your bed or lap, keep your quilting lines farther apart.

2. The matchstick quilting makes a dense, stiff appearance and feel. This much quilting is great for quilts that will be hung on the wall.

3. In this design, she combined different patterns of quilting and mostly ignored the design of the quilt. By creating a strong diagonal and fills of differing shapes and sizes, Mandy created another layer of design. Notice how the quilting patterns are mostly of a similar scale and fairly large, so the effect is still soft and fluffy and would work well on a functional quilt. I am also noticing how the quilt seems less formal to me because of the softness and variety of patterns such as pebbles and the grid.

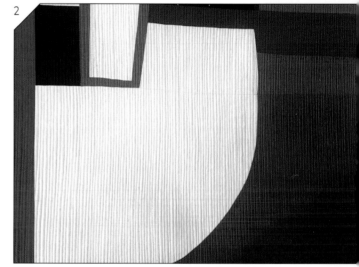

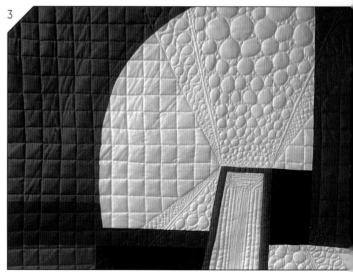

4. The pattern follows the pattern of the quilt, calling attention to and enhancing the design. To add interest, she created a pattern within the quilting pattern of thin and thicker lines in a regular rhythm. Quilting this close together creates a stiff surface, as did the matchstick, and would not be comfy on a bed or lap quilt. I like the way I can imagine the lines as brushstrokes or "combing" in a thick layer of paint.

5. I find it very interesting how whirls and swirls and feathers work on a contemporary designed quilt top. I love how the texture of these ornate patterns changes my view from the color and forms in the design to a focus on only the quilting patterns. The colors and shapes are still there, but to me they are no longer the focus of the finished quilted piece. What do you think? I imagine a very stark, minimal living room sitting on an exquisitely designed antique Turkish carpet. Can they work together to create a harmonious piece, or do they fight for attention, leaving us confused?

6. An edge-to-edge pattern such as this one, often created by using the pantograph rolls on a longarm machine, are quick and easy for quilting. There are thousands of pantograph patterns from which to choose. The trick is to choose the correct one that will work well with your quilt design. Most of the quilts on which this type of quilting is used are functional, and the finished texture is fluffy and cozy. In this example, I am not sure whether or not the pattern really works with the design.

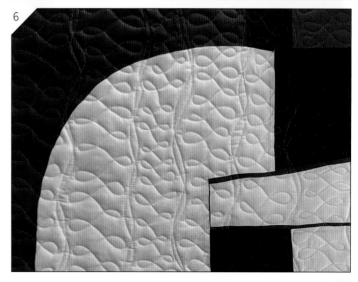

HOW TO TIE A QUILT

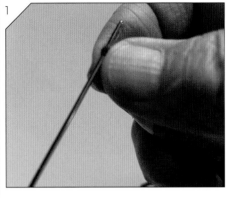

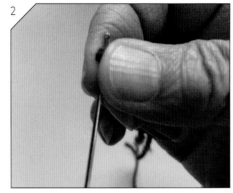

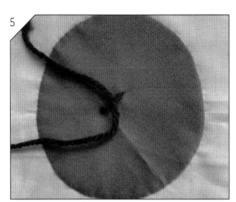

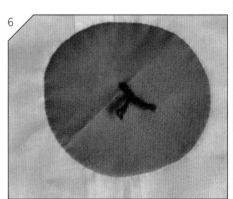

I love to tie my casual, fun quilts. It's fast and easy and makes for a soft and crafty quilt. Here's how to do it . . .

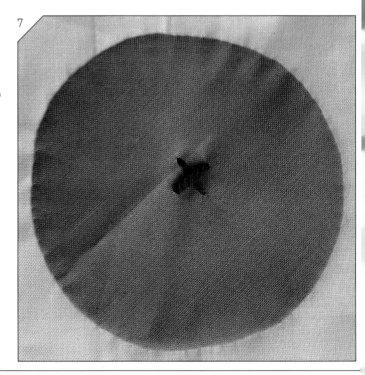

1. The most difficult part of the process is threading the yarn through a needle. Use a tapestry needle with a sharp point. Wrap the yarn over the eye of the needle, pull tight, and squeeze the yarn over the needle. Place the eye of the needle over the folded yarn and push down until the yarn goes through the eye. (1 ,2, 3)

2. To tie, make a large stitch, trim the ends to a couple of inches, and tie in a square knot. Trim to $1/2$" and fluff! (4, 5, 6)

3. For a cleaner look, stitch from the back of the quilt and make a cross-stitch. Tie in a square knot on the back. (7)

BINDING

After our quilts are quilted, the edges need to be finished. Traditionally, a binding was the appropriate way to finish the edges, and no one gave much thought as to how it could be part of the overall design except for color. Today, many modern and art quilts are using a facing on the edges. Of course, there are fussy-cut bindings to consider, pillow-turned edges, and completely unfinished edges for extra artiness!

A traditional binding is a long strip of straight-of-grain or bias-cut fabric sewn onto either the front or the back of the quilt and then folded over the edge and sewn into place. As you can see in the quilts below, this type of binding in a contrasting color creates a frame around the quilt. In a similar color to the background as in the quilt to the right, it creates a subtle, nicely finished edge. I often create a fussy-cut binding to finish my quilts. I love playing with the design all the way to the edge. In the quilt below, Lucinda Walker used her binding as an integral part of the overall design to great effect.

The other edge finish most used is a facing. This is a strip of fabric sewn to the front and turned completely to the back and hand-stitched in place. There are many good tutorials on the internet on how to do a facing. My favorites are on cottonbourbon.com and susanbrubakerknapp.com.

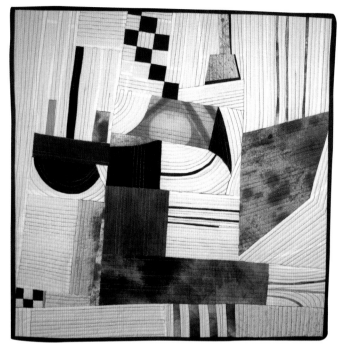

Airport Blues

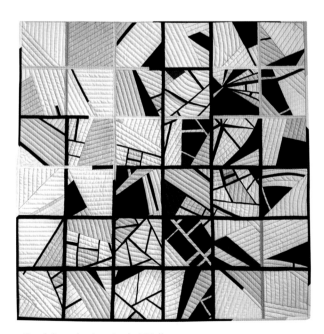

Revisions by Lucinda Walker

Karaoke

IN THE FOLLOWING SECTION, THERE ARE
A SERIES OF EXERCISES THAT WILL HONE
YOUR SKILLS IN THE DESIGN ELEMENTS AND
PRINCIPLES. EVEN IF YOU ARE AN ACCOMPLISHED
ARTIST, PRACTICE IS ALWAYS HELPFUL TO KEEP
YOU PROGRESSING!

DO THEM WHILE YOU ARE TALKING ON THE
PHONE OR WATCHING TV. USE THEM TO FIND NEW
PATTERNS OR NEW IDEAS!

DESIGN EXERCISES
TO HONE YOUR SKILLS

A big question I had when I decided to start writing this book was "How do I teach people to use these concepts?" It's difficult when we are not in the same room or where we can discuss and practice how to think about design in our own work. I studied art for most of my life and didn't realize how much I knew until I started teaching. It dawned on me about two years into teaching that I actually learned things in school! I also realized, though, that I have been drawing and painting and sewing and generally making something almost every day for 68 years. All that practice has made me fearless to try new things. I am not afraid to experiment and push into new directions. I'm a better artist because I have tried and failed and tried again and failed again. I've stuck a paintbrush through a canvas. Ripped a quilt in two. But I keep going and pushing. Is it an obsession? Yes, it is, and I know that. I don't make a choice to make art; I just do it. Every day. And I always have.

It's all the "doing" that keeps me going, and all the practice I am getting while I am actually making something that builds my skills. In order to build your own skills, I suggest making something every day. I suggest getting a sketchbook or two. One large for more-expressive drawings, and one small to keep with you for sketching. Pick out a favorite pen or pencil and start doodling, drawing, making marks. These should be quick sketches, not finished or detailed studies. While you are sketching, you are automatically working on line and shape. Make these into patterns through repetition. Examine texture through different kinds of marks. Draw fruit and learn to see how light and shadow work to depict three-dimensional form.

I also make sewn black-and-white "sketches" to work from. Photographs are an endless way to grab a shape or interesting lines and weird things to play with later. I don't use sketches directly for my quilts, but I see them as guides and inspiration.

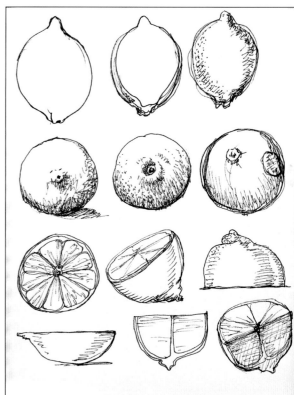

PRACTICE FOR BALANCE

Cut four 4" squares of black paper or fabric and cut four 2" squares of black paper or fabric.

Arrange all or some of these squares on a sheet of white paper to create the following:

(take a photo of each arrangement)

1. Symmetric balance design

2. Asymmetric balance design

3. Equal figure ground relationship (equal amount of black and white)

4. Negative space predominant (mostly white if black is figure)

5. Positive space predominant (mostly black if black is figure)

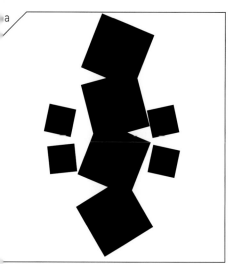

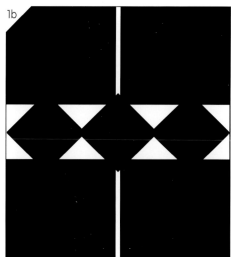

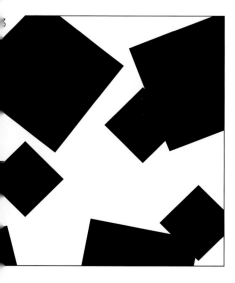

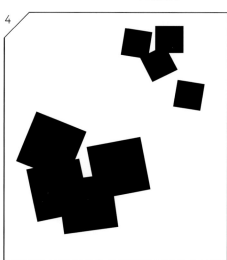

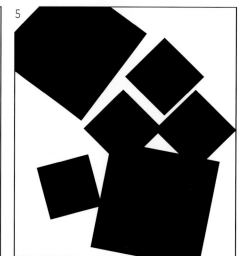

PRACTICE FOR MOVEMENT/RHYTHM

Cut six to eight 1" x 7" strips of black paper or fabric.

1. Arrange the strips to depict an even, slow rhythm.

2. Arrange the strips to depict a staccato rhythm.

3. Draw different rhythms.

4. Find fabrics that express different rhythms—why?

5. What rhythms and movements do these fabrics convey?

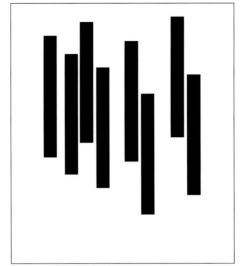

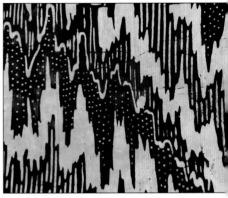

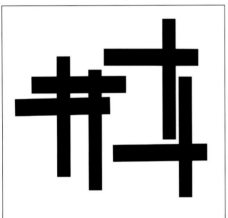

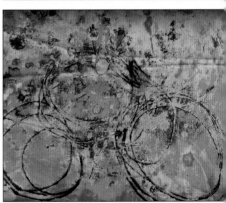

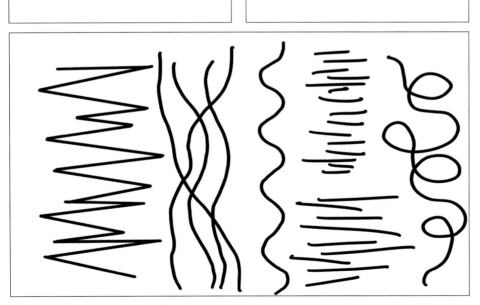

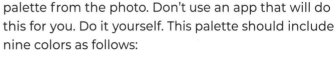

PRACTICE FOR COLOR: CHOOSING A PALETTE

Create a five-color palette that includes the following:

A warm color
A cool color
A tint
A shade
A primary color
A secondary color
A tertiary color
At least one neutral
(Remember that colors change temperature depending on who they're with)

Find a photograph that is not too complicated. Pick a palette from the photo. Don't use an app that will do this for you. Do it yourself. This palette should include nine colors as follows:

1 light value
2 medium-light values
3 medium values
2 medium-dark values
1 dark value

Choose a medium-value color. Using it as the base:

Choose an analogous color palette

Choose a complementary palette

Choose a split-complementary palette

Choose a triadic color palette

PLAYING WITH VALUE

Value is easy to see when it's set up like this, especially in gray scale. It's more difficult to decide values in color. To practice identifying value in colors, pick a color of each value and then take a photograph on your phone in grays cale and see how you did.

The fabrics below were more complicated. I thought I had picked colors that would be easy to value, but I wanted to see where the red ended up. When I turned it to gray scale, I was shocked that the values of the colors are very close.

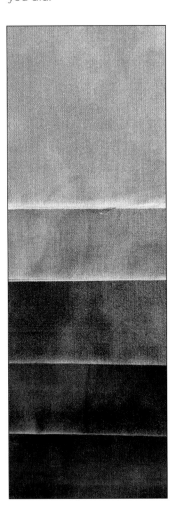 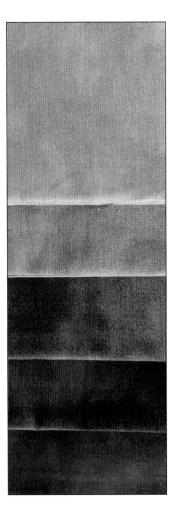

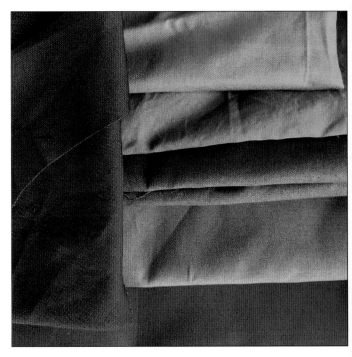

Above, the fabrics I picked out I thought were obvious. I was a bit surprised though at how close in value the darker three fabrics turned out.

AUDITIONING A BACKGROUND COLOR

What a difference color can make! Sometimes it's difficult to decide on a background color for a quilt. In this piece by Janel RItchie, but she couldn't decide what would enhance the design of this improv project. We loaded the image into Adobe Photoshop and played with the choices. Instead of going to a completely different color from those in the quilt, we chose colors that were already in the design to audition.

The dark purple was a rich color that made the pale yellow pop! Yellow is a light-value color and also the complement to purple on the color wheel.

We found it interesting how the light blue brightened the center design and defined its shape better than the dark purple, but it didn't enhance the fun aspect of the quilt.

The yellow is fun and gives the illusion of holes in the design from the yellow design elements. It' s definitely a good choice because it keeps the overall mood light and airy and fun.

The green background just kills the design elements by blending in too much. Even though it's my favorite color, it doesn't always work!

In the end, she decided that a solid color wasn't the correct decision for this piece. She loved how continuing the pattern made the quilt sing!

HOW TO DESIGN: SOME EXAMPLES AND THOUGHTS!

This brings us to the crux of the matter. Can you show us how to design a quilt using the design principles that will always be successful? Probably not. It's difficult to explain how this all works. As I've said earlier in the book, creating art is about tapping into intuition and having a conversation with your materials and other artists, not following rules. When the rules are all that matter, the creativity takes a back seat in the process. As you carefully make all your triangle points line up perfectly and you study the color wheel to verify that yes, indeedy, orange is the complement of royal blue, not yellow, what is lost? The spontaneity and passion are replaced by strict adhesure to "what works." Your individual opinion on whether that yellow is great with that rich deep blue—and your trust in your own taste is what drives the creative spirit. Not a color wheel. The passion is replaced by a sense of uninspired lifelessness. Is this a bit harsh? Yep. But I want to make my point that what makes YOUR art special and successful is YOU, not some set of guidelines thought up in 1930 at a completely different time in the world.

I'm going to try, though, to talk you through some decisions I've made when making my own quilts. What was I thinking? I often wonder that myself!

Let's look at *Twitter*. This quilt began as two large pieces of black fabric I had already cut out to use in another quilt. The shape on the left was purposely cut out for the quilt on the right below, (the figure with the three windows), but the figure on the right was a leftover piece of black. The big circle on the "head" of the left figure was cut out from an earlier quilt as was the little stack of squares. Even the big white "eye" circles with color were cut from another piece. I just arranged them on the wall.

I positioned the two big shapes carefully to have a "sexy" space between them. I wanted them to be having a conversation. Why does one have "legs"? I don't know. I was pulling out scraps and placing them in places that made sense at the time. Long legs vs little short legs? The big circular shape seemed heavy and I found another white circle left over to thin it out. The squares didn't make any sense at this juncture, so I found those big fat linear scraps and made the top of the head for the right-side figure. Where did that "Mohawk" hair come from? A big scrap with short strips of black. Everything I put on the wall was a scrap from the three previous quilts. Even though just scraps, I placed them very carefully in order to create the relationships of figure and background that "felt" right. Should the top of the headpiece on the right figure sit directly on the body shape? I tried that . . .too blocky and heavy. Do they balance each other? Through trial and error, I placed, scootched, replaced until the black shapes were looking good —fun and in conversation. (1)

Then the colors needed to be laid in. I looked around the studio at my bins and the yellows looked good. What works with yellow? Well, purple is its complement. Did I think through that? No. I just chose what "felt" right to me on that day. The figure on the right could have been red but I was tired of red. Green was too much the same as the yellows and oranges. Turquoise could have worked just fine the figure on the left could have been purple and the one on the right yellow. All these would have worked just as well as what I ended up using. I was in the mood for these two colors that day. (2, 3, 4)

I laid in the scraps of color, not paying much attention but pulling out fabrics from the "orange-yellow" bin and the "purple" bin. Definitely needed some red to brighten everything up, so added that. The "Mohawk" hair was orange at some point but felt too matchy-matchy, so I pulled out the greens. (5)

As I added color to the figures, I began filling in the background. I chose various values of grays to offset the brightly colored figures. I had learned from Nancy Crow that yellow is always a light! I threw some on the wall and loved the way the entire piece began to sparkle. (6)

As I took the scraps off the wall to sew them together, I started realizing that I loved the black and the definition and depth it provided. I thought long and hard and in the end decided to leave parts of the figures black. My true love is those thin line details, and that's when the figures became birds. I loved the white against the black, the thin lines against the large sections of color. I like that the details defined the personalities of the figures.

DOES THIS EXPLAIN HOW THIS PIECE CAME TOGETHER AS FAR AS DESIGN PRINCIPLES?

I think it is balanced through color and arrangement. I have used color and value to create depth and definition. I used color theory so that the colors zing. It's unified through technique and subject matter but has variety. Why does the left bird float off the ground, and why does that work? I can't really say, but It feels right to me. When they became birds, the attributions of birds bring some sense into it.

In this quilt, you can see I began with leftovers. Some of the scraps already have been drawn on! As usual, I just started arranging on my wall. (1)

I fill in spaces with found shapes, paying attention to size more than anything else for this one. I put things up, move them around, add more. (2)

Fill in empty spaces with more scraps. Slabs of fabric that seem too large get cut into shapes. I instinctively balance the color across the surface. (3)

The yellows seems to be important, and the light blue gray is a nice neutral. The "circles" are carefully tilted to be playful, not structured along an axis. (4)

I remember placing the "bumps" and reds very strategically! (5)

Mark Makers Spin

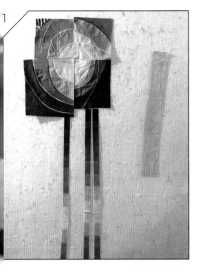

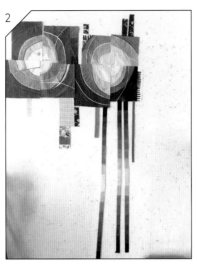

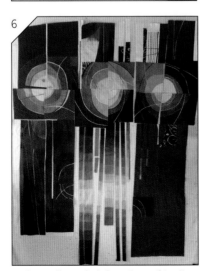

The *Guardian Quilts* all began with the large circular shapes. Four quarter circles constructed from different fabrics and inundated with thin lines placed near the top of the quilt. I had taken a dyeing class from Malka Dubrowsky and had made value studies on half yards of fabric. I was fascinated by the way they created a "shine" when lined up in strips.

You can see that I started with one circle on stilts. I began to add scrap strips to add interest. (1, 2)

At one point I had decided to play with the edges of the squared-off circles. Those looked too much like "fins," so I took them off and used solids. (3)

That was too heavy. In the photo on the left, you can tell that the dark blues are taking over the design, so I separated them. I also felt the valued striped fabric was too prominent. Instead of using it as a solid piece, I cut it into more strips. When these strips are arranged on top of a white ground, they create the glow instead of just a stripe. (4)

At this point, the large blocks of blues needed to be lightened, and as I separated them from each other, they became "bodies" or columns. You can see how I kept adding details to break up large areas of color and added the warm colors to balance out the color. (5)

The top center hand-dyed fabric was distracting to me. I added blue strips into it to break up the awkward space. The finished piece is well balanced with interesting figures. The background creates a rhythm across the surface. The repeat of circles in the big blue areas brings the viewer's eyes down and creates interest. (6)

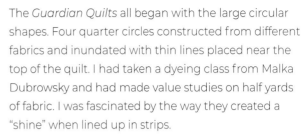

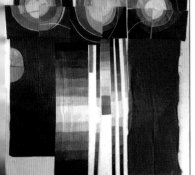

Guardian, Celebration of Indigo

Viola de Gamba started with two large hand-dyed fabrics. I loved the ombre effect and the texture. I wanted to show off the fabric by leaving large shapes of it. (1)

I created the center stripes with ombre strips of the red orange and grays, not sure what would come next. (2)

I threw on the green rectangle that was in the scrap pile. I loved the green with the gray. This color palette is striking because of the values. (3)

I used scraps from cutting out the large curved shapes and two tiny pieces of Japanese antique floral fabric for fun. Notice how the long, thin lines fill the empty space on the left and balance the large half circles. The lines create a different "sound" and rhythm than the large, sonorous shapes. (4)

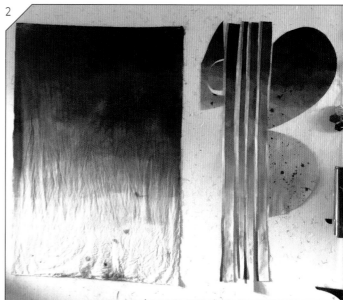

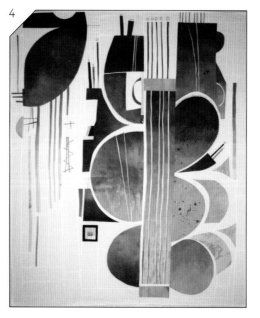

Viola da Gamba

COMMON THINGS TO WATCH FOR

These are the most-common design issues I see in my workshops. Even if we know all the rules and we are carefully following them, some slip through the cracks. Often it's because we are concentrating so hard on something else that we forget to step back and study our designs as a whole.

1. Value mistakes

One of the most common issues I see is that bright colors are not considered by value. Color and value are separate from each other, and brights are mostly a medium value. Let's look at this Marcia Derse fabric. Beautiful colors! We know they will work together because they are from the same line/designer. Right? Not necessarily. Even though the colors are very different, look at the values! These bright colors will always read as medium value. Your quilt will pop with color but also be muddy and flat because value provides depth and contrast. (1a, 1b)

2. Difference in scale and placement

In the drawing on the left, all the figures are equal in size/scale. They create the illusion that all of them are in the same plane and in a line. This arrangement fails to create a sense of depth, even though they are different colors and values. The characters in the right-hand drawing are different sizes and positions. One is larger, two overlap. They create an illusion of depth and movement by their size and placement. Even though the blue figure "should" recede because it is a cool color, it is placed a bit lower and overlaps the green guy and therefore reads as closer to us. The big orange dude should look closer to us because of his size. But, no, because of where he is placed on the line, we know he is not as close as the blue guy. (2a, 2b)

3. Sexy spacing

I often see students place components too far apart. The secret to "sexy" spacing is that space where the objects almost touch, but not quite. They seem to have magnets in them that are drawing them together, but the anticipation of their touching is exquisite. Think of all the couple sitcoms that created sexual tension between the main characters. We watched for the moment they would actually admit it! But, alas, once it actually occurred, the tension was gone and

the series would inevitably come to an end. The rectangles on the left are almost touching, creating a relationship between them. The spaces in the diagram on the left are very interesting as well. When you look at the diagram on the right, the figures are too far apart and don't seem to be talking to each other. They are hanging around in the same field but may or may not have a relationship. The negative space between them is also not as interesting. (3a, 3b)

4. Lack of movement and lack of zing!

I made these two quilts a few years back but never liked either of them. They lacked movement and zing. There wasn't anything interesting enough in them to hold my attention. I think too often that we make quilts and decide they are "okay," but unless we feel the magic when we are making them, the quilts themselves won't have any magic in them. (4a, 4b)

5. Tentative relationships

In the quilt, everything is a muddle. The shapes don't relate in any interesting way, and the color arrangements don't make sense. It's a big mess in every way! I was trying too hard to use all the fabric I had made in a fabric-dyeing workshop. (5)

6. Lack of contrast

This quilt which I made, is not a bad quilt by any means. It is lacking something though. The values are muddy. They do create a sense of the murky deeps as I wanted, but not in an interesting way. It would have been stronger with more attention to value and contrast. (6a, 6b)

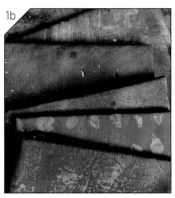

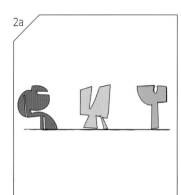

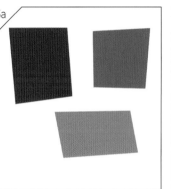

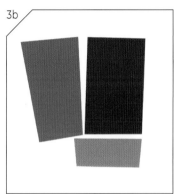

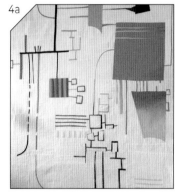

INSPIRATION TO DRAW ON

On the next pages are photographs of the quilts I have made from June 2021 through August 2023. I love seeing them in one place and noticing how they grow and shift as my circumstances change. I'm not an artist who consciously works in series, but I make what appeals to me at any given time. There are motifs that are evident throughout the work, but also differences. I am easily distracted by new fabrics or new colors or new spaces and walls on which to create, and you will see that. I also was influenced by my workshop with Nancy Crow when I began making large shapes. I tried to make them with my own voice over the next year, and I am very happy with the work I did after that (October 2021). I notice that large circles are one of my favorite things, and I keep coming back to them.

Old Friends

Tryst

The Nanny

Top Hats and Hash Tags

Conversation

Hi How Are You?

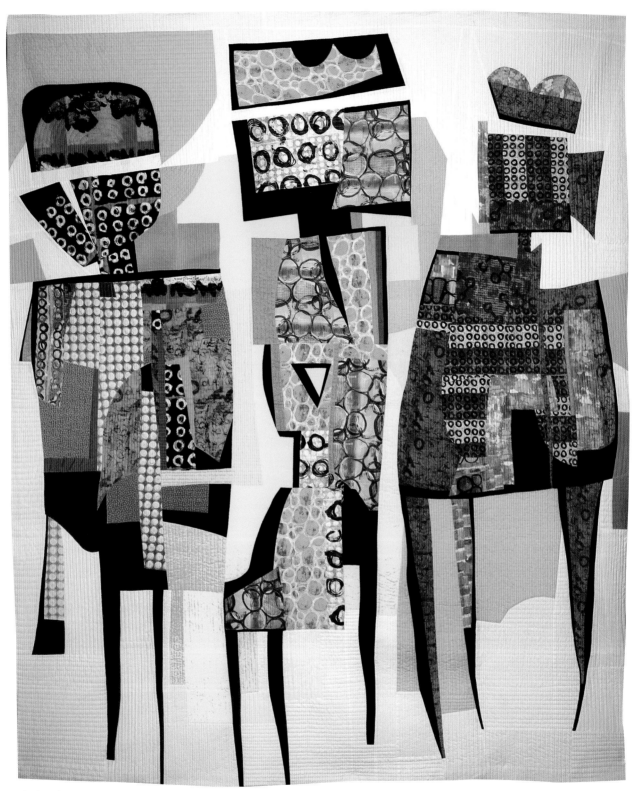

Attitude

Tense Talk

Minty Peach Fuzz

Clandestine

Desperados

Facets

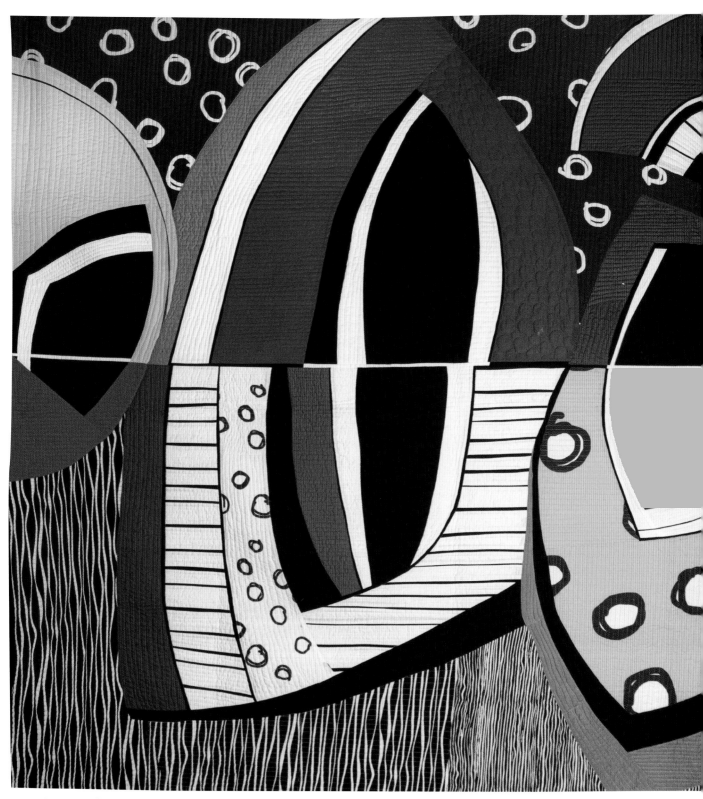

Party Conversation

Facets

Hearth

Grace 1: Play

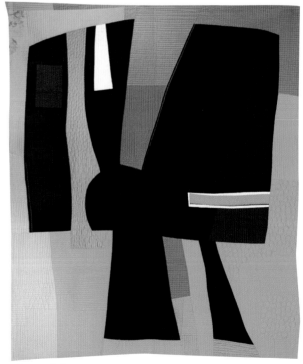

Grace 2: Joy

Grace 3: Imperfection

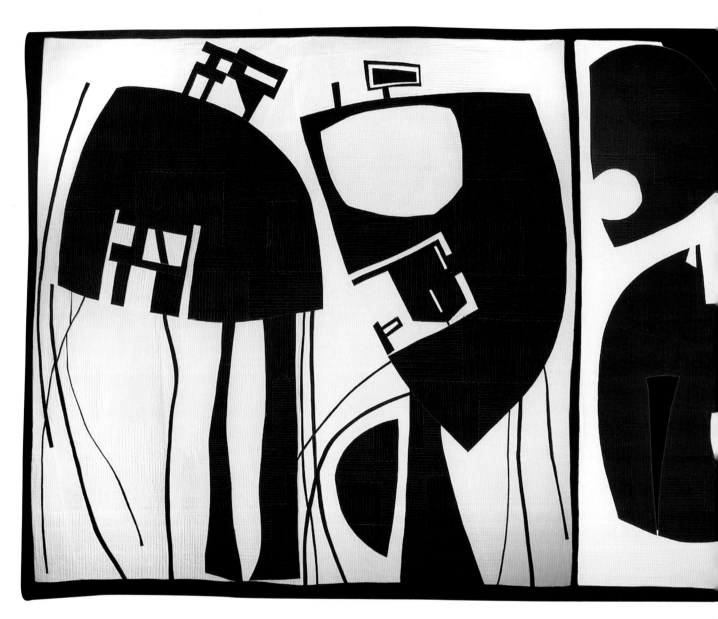

Chatter

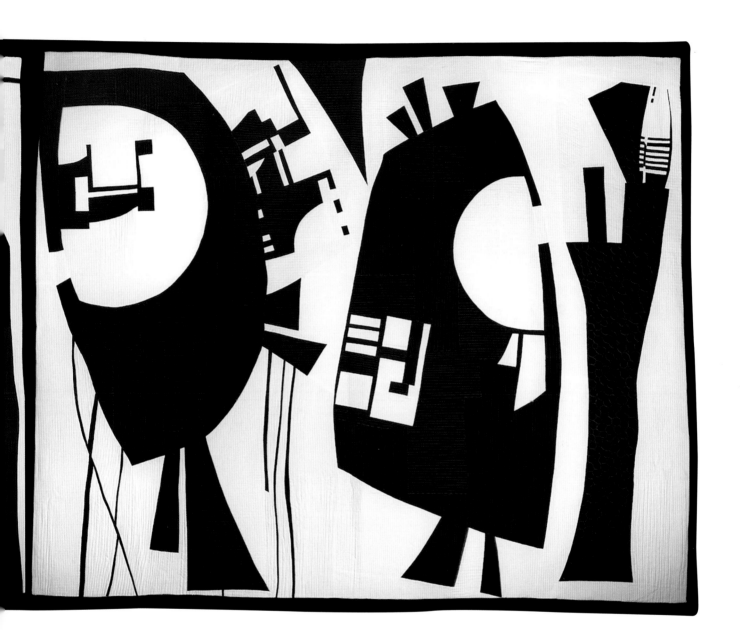

Flourish

Bloom

SUGGESTED READING

There are thousands of books and websites and fiber artists available to us. I can't possibly find them all or even tell you which ones I've looked at and used in my quilt practice to date. Here are just a few I have in my library that I recommend:

FOR IMPROV

Grisdela, Cindy. *Adventures in Improv: Master Color, Design & Construction.* C&T Publishing, 2021.

———. *Artful Improv: Explore Color Recipes, Building Blocks & Free-Motion Quilting.* C&T Publishing, 2016.

Shell, Maria. *Improv Patchwork: Dynamic Quilts Made with Line and Shape.* Stash Books, 2017.

Wood, Sherri Lynn. *The Improv Handbook for Modern Quilters: A Guide to Creating, Quilting and Living Courageously.* STC Craft, 2015.

FOR QUILTING

Cameli, Christina. *Free-Motion Combinations: Unlimited Quilting Designs.* C&T Publishing, 2021.

Fons, Marianne, and Liz Porter. *Quilter's Complete Guide.* Dover, 2020.

Gering, Jacquie. *Walk: Master Machine Quilting with Your Walking Foot.* Lucky Spool Media, 2016.

———. *Walk 2.0: More Machine Quilting with Your Walking Foot.* Lucky Spool Media, 2020.

FOR COLOR

Albers, Joseph. *Interaction of Color.* Yale University Press, 1977.

Batchelor, David. *Chromophobia.* Reaktion Books, 2000.

Hornung, David. *Color. A Workshop for Artists and Designers.* Laurence King, 2012.

Thomas, Heather. *A Fiber Artist's Guide to Color and Design: The Basics & Beyond.* Landauer, 2011.

Wolfrom, Joen. *Color Play—Easy Steps to Imaginative Color in Quilts.* C&T Publishing, 2000.

FOR DESIGN

Barton, Elizabeth. *Inspired to Design: Seven Steps to Successful Art Quilts.* C&T Publishing, 2013.

Doughty, Kathy. *Organic Appliqué: Creative Hand-Stitching Ideas and Techniques.* Stash Books, 2019.

Marston, Gwen. *Liberated Quiltmaking.* American Quilters Society, 1997.

FOR INSPIRATION

All books by and about Nancy Crow.

All books by Gwen Marston.

Arnett, William. The *Quilts of Gee's Bend: Masterpieces from a Lost Place.* Tinwood, 2003.

Crow, Nancy. *Nancy Crow: Improvisational Quilts.* C&T Publishing, 1996.

Cunningham, Joe. *Men and the Art of Quiltmaking.* American Quilter's Society, 2010.

Kiracofe, Roderick. *Unconventional & Unexpected: American Quilts below the Radar, 1950–2000.* STC Craft, 2014. rev. 2nd ed., Schiffer, 2022.

Schmied Wieland. *Friedensreich Hundertwasser, 1928–2000.* Taschen GmbH, 2014.